INTRODUCTORY LOGIC
AND
FORMAL METHODS

Formal methods are becoming of increasing importance and are now part of most Computer Science degree courses. This textbook is primarily intended for 2nd or 3rd Year undergraduate students on such courses.

The emphasis in any formal specification language is on rigour and hence Computer Scientists must be familiar with the rudiments of both logic and discrete mathematics. Consequently, the particular focus of this book is to introduce the essential elements of logic and also a particular formal specification language, **Z**.

INTRODUCTORY LOGIC AND FORMAL METHODS

David Heath
University of Luton

Derek Allum
University of Luton

Lynne Dunckley
University of Luton

ALFRED WALLER LIMITED
HENLEY-ON-THAMES

Published by
Alfred Waller Ltd, Publishers
Orchards, Fawley, Henley-on-Thames
Oxfordshire RG9 6JF

First published 1994

British Library Catologuing-in-
Publication Data
A catalogue record for this book is
available from the British Library

ISBN 1 872474 10 1

Produced for the publishers by
John Taylor Book Ventures
Hatfield, Herts

Printed and bound in Great Britain by
The Lavenham Press
Lavenham Suffolk

Contents

5 An Introduction to Z

6 Propositional and predicate calculus

11 An Introduction to Proofs in Z

12 Z-Developments and Variations

Appendix A A music library specification

1

Introduction and Overview

1.1 Introduction

The formalisation of mathematics arose out of the initial requirement to make precise the notion of number, leading to the development of the number system as we know it today. The process of formalisation can thus be regarded as making vague ideas precise.

Mathematics provides the foundation upon which software development using **formal methods** is based. The philosophy of this approach is to use mathematics as a vehicle with which to deliver precision and clarity. In the process of obtaining this clarification, difficult decisions about the requirements of the system being modelled have to be taken rather than avoided. These design decisions can then be captured in mathematics and formalised.

The aim of this initial chapter is to 'set the scene' for what follows. In particular, we discuss the following:

♦ the requirements of a formal specification

♦ the mathematical underpinning of **Z**

♦ a simple, introductory **Z** schema

1.2 Why formal methods?

It is becoming increasingly apparent that an appreciation and understanding of the rudiments of logic and formal specification are of the utmost importance in computer science. For example, logic at its simplest level in terms of truth tables is used in the design of computer architecture. Also, an understanding of simple logical concepts is involved in forming compound conditions in high level programming languages. These simple examples illustrate the practical usefulness of logic in computer science.

Demand for 'high-integrity' software has arisen in a range of industries. Software is unsatisfactory for two major reasons: either it does not do what the user wants or it tries to do the correct thing but fails. To solve the first of these problems we need a precise specification. If the specification is not precise, the software may not truly reflect the user requirements. Given a precise specification, we can develop software using rigorous methods, which facilitate the solution of the second problem as well as the first.

1.3 Fundamental aspects of formal methods

Engineers in more traditional and well established disciplines have long been in the habit of collecting all the relevant data about an existing system and its behaviour. Mathematical principles have then been introduced to describe the relationships between the various factors operating, since these may influence the course of the investigation. The results of this analysis are used to construct a mathematical model of the system which represents the problem to be solved. Detailed designs are then based on the theoretical model.

In the same way, the objective in using formal methods for software development is to express the essential features of the system, while at the same time removing unnecessary details which obscure the fundamental logical rules operating in the system. The choice of the word 'methods' in the title *formal methods* is to reflect the fact that it gives a methodology for tackling specification problems.

Now, more than ever before, there is a requirement to produce specifications from which software can be accurately produced. The use of any natural language to specify the requirements of a piece of software immediately allows the possibility of ambiguities being introduced, since the same words can be interpreted differently by different people. For this reason, formal methods of specification which rely heavily on mathematics and logic have been developed to provide a framework and a specialised language of their own to enable precise software specification.

There are, moreover, two further important advantages of using formal methods. Firstly, the replacement of a natural language by a mathematical specification imposes precision and also allows the possibility of proving that the end product is correct. Secondly, if the problem is defined mathematically, we can use mathematical techniques to derive results about the problem as we have described it. This is absolutely essential as we must be able to test the proposed model of the system to find out if it is in fact consistent and whether the deductions we make from it are correct and accurate.

In this textbook, the aim is to provide the undergraduate studying computer science with the important elements of logic and predicate calculus required for an understanding and appreciation of formal methods. It is a large subject area and, hence, in this textbook the particular formal specification language **Z** developed by the Programming Research Group at Oxford University is studied in detail.

1.4 The requirements of a formal specification

The purpose of a formal specification is to provide an expression of precisely what a desired software system should do without stating how these actions will be achieved. A formal specification thus places no constraint upon the system design or implementation.

To summarise, a formal specification should:

a)   open up a range of formal solutions

b)   only contain the crucial aspects of the system requirements

c)   not contain any ambiguity which introduces scope for errors

d)   be partitioned into discrete sections which make little or no reference to other parts of the document. In **Z**, this is achieved by the use of 'schemas' which are self-contained and are used to specify individual operations and states

It has also been suggested that, ideally, the formal specification should be understandable by the client. To what extent this may be possible is open to debate. It is impractical to expect an accountant or a busy manager to commit time to reach the necessary level of familiarisation. The mathematical theory behind formal methods is not particularly difficult but, clearly, to use it as a communication tool may need some parallel education for the user community. Where communication can improve, is where the rigour of the specification method will make the computer specialist check particular points when inconsistencies of interpretation are revealed.

It is also a mistake to consider that formal methods will replace natural language. It has, for example, become good practice among systems analysts to discuss with the users the specification that is produced by the analysts, so that some agreement can be reached and errors detected in good time. This means that a formal specification needs translation to ensure the user gains understanding of what is proposed. This might take the form of some explanatory natural language text to accompany the mathematics. Consequently, natural language will still be used within the specification to provide clarity of exposition and to link the mathematics together in order to produce a more readable document.

1.5 An informal introduction to Z schemas

The purpose of this section is to provide a flavour of what is meant by a **Z schema** rather than a rigorous introduction to what is admittedly a difficult subject. It is hoped that this will set the scene for the rest of the book and emphasise some of the mathematical underpinning required for a study of **Z**. To this end, let us consider the specification of a system for a small bookshop.

In order to develop this example, we will draw on two basic mathematical notions:

    (i) the concept of a set

    (ii) the concept that one item may be related to another item

These ideas are fundamental to modern mathematics. Students, who are unfamiliar with these basic ideas, are advised to defer a full understanding of them until chapter 2 where they are dealt with in greater depth.

In this introductory example, we will not consider all of the operations that could be required in a bookshop such as purchasing a book, restocking and querying stock levels. Instead we will concentrate on the fundamental relations which hold between the entities with which the bookshop deals, such as books, where they are physically held within the bookshop and the stockholding of each book.

In its simplest terms, a set can be defined as a collection of objects. The elements of each set are conventionally enclosed in curly brackets so that we write, for example, $A == \{1, 2, 3\}$. This defines a set, A, consisting of three numbers. The use of the double equals sign here (==) is used to emphasise that it is a definition. The concept of a set and the various operations relating to sets will, however, be defined in greater detail in chapter 2.

We introduce and define a set, called *Book*, which consists of **all** published titles. Each published book is uniquely identified by its ISBN number with all the copies of a particular edition of a book, such as Tolkien's *'Lord of the Rings'*, having the same ISBN number. Typical ISBN numbers are: 0-216-90488-9, 0-471-09373-4, 0-14-012501-9. Consequently, we define the finite set *Book* as consisting of all ISBN numbers so that:

Book == {0-216-90488-9, 0-471-09373-4, 0-14-012501-9, ...}

where the dots indicate that the definition of the set by listing its contents is incomplete.

The bookshop will hold books on bookshelves. Our simplified method of identifying or 'labelling' the bookshelves is to give each shelf a numeric code. Accordingly, we introduce the set, *Place,* containing the set of shelf identifiers used by the bookshop which, for the purposes of illustration, we take as 1 to 10. Hence, we have:

Place == {1, 2, 3, 4, 5, 6, 7, 8, 9, 10}

The operation of the system is controlled by the schema, *BookShop,* which relates the basic sets comprising the system. Before we specify this illustrative schema, we will introduce and define the standard set, N_1, which consists of all the natural counting numbers commencing with one. The definition of this is given by:

N_1 == {1, 2, 3, 4, 5, ...}

where the dots indicate that it has no end. Technically, such sets are called **infinite** by mathematicians to emphasise that they do not terminate.

The concept of a **relation** between members of sets can now be developed using the two sets *Book* and *Place* already introduced. Clearly, there is a relation between a book and the bookshelf on which it is located. Since each bookshelf is identified by a unique identifier belonging to the set *Place* we can state there is a relation between each member of *Book* held by the bookshop and each member of *Place.* The particular notation used in **Z** to denote such a relation is the bi-directional arrow ↔, so that we can write:

Book ↔ *Place*

This may be read as '*Book* is related to *Place* '. In such a relationship, the set on the left of the bi-directional arrow is referred to as the **source** and the set on the right as the **target**. The items of the source which are involved in the relation are referred to as the **domain**, and the corresponding items of the target set are referred to as the **range**. In the illustrative example we are considering here, the domain is not the same as the source as there will be many books for which the bookshop has no demand and hence has no stockholding. For ease of reference, we can give a meaningful name to this relation. The relation between *Book* and *Place* we will call *storage* and we write:

storage : *Book* ↔ *Place*

This relationship can be shown diagrammatically below in Fig. 1.1 which shows the difference between the terms source and domain, and also the difference between target and range. We note from Fig. 1.1 that, in this example, the source contains the domain and the target contains the range.

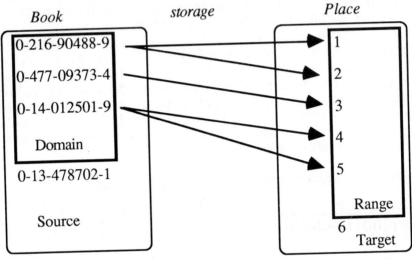

Fig. 1.1 The relation *storage*

In this figure books with the following ISBN numbers 0-216-90488-9, 0-471-09373-4, 0-14-012501-9 are currently in stock, whilst those with any other ISBN number such as 0-13-478702-1 are not currently in stock.

We can now introduce the basic schema for the bookshop and explain each line of it in detail afterwards:

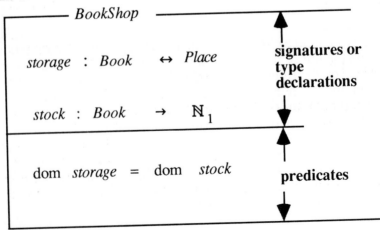

Fig. 1.2 A typical **Z** schema

The name of this schema is *BookShop*. The first thing to note about schemas is that they are usually divided into two sections. The first section contains **signatures,** which are also sometimes called **type declarations,** which define the types of the relations introduced. These two terms are synonymous. The second section of the schema contains **predicates** or **propositions** about the declarations in the first part.

The meaning of the lines in this schema are now explained. The two lines in the first part of the schema block declare two relations which we expect to hold. The first relation, *storage,* has already been explained in some detail. The second line in the schema introduces a special type of relation known as a **function** which in this case is called, *stock,* and is given by:

$$stock : Book \rightarrow \mathbb{N}_1$$

which relates *Book* to the set $\mathbb{N}_1$ of natural numbers.

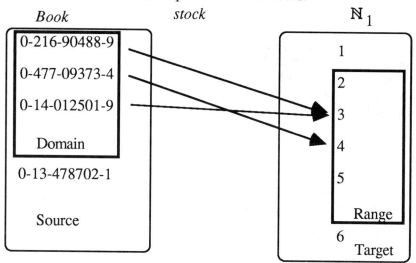

Fig. 1.3   The function *stock*

For each particular ISBN number held by the bookshop there will be a number of copies. The function *stock* relates the ISBN number to the appropriate quantity in $\mathbb{N}_1$ to indicate the number of copies held. For example, the book with ISBN number 0-216-90488-9 has a stockholding of three copies. A book which is not currently in stock has no stockholding and does not participate in the function as the target set $\mathbb{N}_1$ consists of integers greater than zero.

The reader should note that the bi-directional arrow is reserved for a relation while the single arrow, →, is used for a function connecting a given domain with its range. Chapters 3 and 4 deal with functions and relations in detail. Meanwhile, we can view a function as a special type of relation connecting one value in the domain to a unique value in the range.

The second section of the introductory schema given above contains only one line. In this line, **dom** is an abbreviation for **domain**. Domain is a technical term which we will consider in detail later but here it can be taken as a list of allowed values. This line expresses that in this system the domain of *storage* is exactly the same as that of *stock* with the result that each item held in store must have a stockholding.

1.6 Summary

This introductory chapter has indicated why formal methods are important and why they should be studied by undergraduates studying computer science.

It has also highlighted, by way of an introductory **Z** schema, the mathematical underpinning required for a study of **Z** without, however, providing a thorough and rigorous introduction to these concepts. Chapter 2 provides a more detailed introduction to sets, which form the foundation and basis of **Z**.

2

Mathematical Preliminaries

2.1 Introduction

The purpose of this chapter is to introduce a number of fundamental concepts that provide the mathematical framework for the work which will be introduced and developed subsequently. A brief and informal overview of some of these concepts was given in chapter 1 but it is now necessary to discuss them in more depth. The starting point is **set theory** which has been called part of 'modern mathematics' although the ideas go back well into the nineteenth century. However, what is used in **Z** is a special version of the set theory that is usually encountered, known as **typed** set theory.

Typed set theory mirrors the way in which objects are organised and collected together in everyday life. For instance, we frequently place items of the same kind together. Public libraries hold separate collections of books and music cassettes, while paintings are held in art galleries. In each case, we have a set of items of 'the same kind'. These examples illustrate that the idea of a typed set is not new, but, in reality it is an organisational principle that we have long accepted. In order to develop an understanding and appreciation of typed set theory, we formally define the following key ideas:

♦ the concept of a set

♦ set membership

♦ subsets

♦ set operations - union, intersection and set difference

♦ set comprehension

♦ power sets

together with some other important operations and ideas which are essential underpinning for an understanding of **Z**. In particular, we additionally introduce the following:

♦ predicates

♦ conjunction and disjunction of predicates

which are essential concepts for the development of set comprehension. However, at this stage in the text, we consider predicates informally and leave a more formal treatment of them until chapter 6.

2.2 Sets

The notion of a **set** is fundamental to much of modern mathematics. Briefly, we may define a set as:

a collection of well defined objects

Each object belonging to the set is an **element** of the set. Moreover, in typed set theory, each element must have the same type. In this sense, the typed set theory used in **Z** is more restrictive than the form in common use, which allows for objects of any type to be placed in the set.

In this text we will in some cases follow the convention of representing a set by a single capital letter apart from those cases where it is more useful to use a meaningful name to reflect the contents of the set. Moreover, as we have already seen in chapter 1, the elements of the set will be placed in curly brackets and will be separated by commas as in the illustrative set $\{1, 2\}$. The curly brackets will be placed on the right hand side of a double equal sign and the name of the set on the left hand side. The double equal sign is used in **Z** when a set is first introduced and defined. Hence, the set *FirstPrimes* containing the first six prime numbers is written as:

FirstPrimes == $\{2, 3, 5, 7, 11, 13\}$

It is worth noting that the order of elements within a set is irrelevant. Two sets consisting of the same elements but in a different order are identical, so that we can write:

$\{1, 2\} = \{2, 1\}$

where, in this case, a single equal sign is used to denote equality.

Moreover, the definition given above does not exclude the possibility of more than one occurrence of an element in a set although, in practice, it is omitted since the duplication is unnecessary and adds nothing to the definition of the set. Hence, we can quite validly write:

$\{1, 2\} = \{1, 2, 2\}$

Although the examples already given show sets with numbers in them, there is no reason why other entities should not be used to define a set.

For example, we could have a set, *Days*, containing the days of the week:

Days == {*Sunday, Monday, Tuesday, Wednesday, Thursday,*
          Friday, Saturday}

In each case, as we would expect in typed set theory, the sets *FirstPrimes* and *Days* each consist of elements of the same kind.

The sets *FirstPrimes* and *Days* are examples of finite **typed sets**. We can also have infinite typed sets as shown in the following examples:

$\mathbb{N}$ == {0, 1, 2, 3, 4, 5, 6, ...} the set of **natural counting numbers**

where the dots, as in chapter 1, indicate that the set continues indefinitely and is an infinite set.

$\mathbb{Z}$ == {..., -3, -2, -1, 0, 1, 2, 3, ...} the set of **all integers**

where, in this case, the dots indicate that the pattern continues indefinitely in both directions. The set $\mathbb{Z}$ is the only built-in type used in **Z** and defines the basic type **integer**.

The definition of the set, $\mathbb{Z}$, illustrates the principle that a **maximal type** contains *all* items with the same characteristic in common. In the case of the set $\mathbb{Z}$, the common characteristic of each element of the set is the property of being an integer. In contrast, although each member of the set $\mathbb{N}$ is also an integer, $\mathbb{N}$ itself is not classed as a maximal type as it does not include every single integer.

2.3 Set membership

The concept of 'belonging' to a set is fundamental: either an element is a member or it is not a member of the set. There is a shorthand notation used to represent set membership. From the definition of the set *Days* in section 2.2 we see that *Sunday* is an element belonging to it. The symbol, $\in$, is used to represent the property of set membership and so we write

Sunday $\in$ *Days*

in which the element is placed on the left hand side and the set to which the element belongs is placed on the right hand side.

Consider now two additional sets, *WeekDays* and *WeekEnd*, given by

WeekDays == {*Monday, Tuesday, Wednesday, Thursday, Friday*}

WeekEnd == {*Saturday, Sunday*}

The symbol $\notin$ is used to represent the property of not belonging to a set. For example, we have

Saturday $\notin$ *WeekDays*

since *Saturday* is not a member of the set *WeekDays*.

It is important to note that the element to be tested for membership must be an element of the underlying type of the set. For this reason, a statement such as

June $\in$ *WeekDays*

is invalid rather than false.

2.4 Subsets

The IBM compatible personal computer (PC) has a number of different graphics cards that it can use. The Hercules and the CGA were two of the earliest, followed in more recent times by the EGA and VGA graphics cards which give a greater variety of colours.

Consider the set *Hercules* == {*black, white*} consisting of the colours available for the Hercules graphics card. The set of colours for the CGA graphics screen is given by *CGA* == {*black, cyan, magenta, white*}. The relationship between these sets is such that *Hercules* is said to be a **proper subset** of *CGA* because *Hercules* is contained in *CGA* and not equal to *CGA*. This is usually represented as

Hercules $\subset$ *CGA*

This notation implies that there are other subsets. If, however, we write

EGA $\subseteq$ *VGA*

we are allowing the possibility that the subset *EGA* may be the entire set *VGA* where, in this case, *EGA* is the set of colours for the EGA graphics screen and *VGA* the colours for the VGA graphics screen. In this case, *EGA* is referred to as a **subset** of *VGA* rather than a proper subset.

2.5 The empty set

There is a special set called the empty set which is denoted by $\emptyset$ and which has the property of 'emptiness' so that it contains no element. The function of this set can be compared to the necessity for zero in arithmetic: it exists in order to make the operations that can be performed on sets complete. However, since as we shall see in section 2.6, these operations can only work on sets of the same type, there is an empty set corresponding to each type. We can explicitly define $\emptyset$ in the form $\emptyset == \{\}$.

2.6 Set operations

There are a number of operations which can be performed on sets. However, in the more restricted environment of typed set theory, these operations can *only* be performed on sets of the same type. The result of each of these operations is yet another set of the same type. Initially, we will illustrate these operations by examples and treat them informally, but, later on when the more difficult topic of set comprehension has been covered, we will give a formal definition of each operation.

The first of such operations is the **union** of two sets. For the purposes of illustration consider the two sets, A and B, each of the same type given below:

$A == \{2, 4, 6, 8\}$ and $B == \{1, 3, 5, 6, 7, 8, 9\}$

Set A consists of the even positive numbers less than 10, while set B contains an assortment of numbers less than 10. The union of the two sets, which is defined as the result of combining A with B with duplicates only occurring once, is written as $A \cup B$ so that

$A \cup B = \{1, 2, 3, 4, 5, 6, 7, 8, 9\}$

The concept of the union of two sets, $A \cup B$, can be illustrated by means of a Venn diagram in which each set is represented by a circle as shown below:

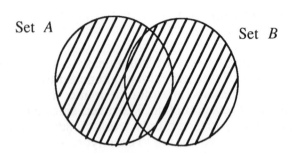

Set A   Set B

Fig. 2.1   The shaded area represents the union
of the two sets.

The sets A and B have an area in common as shown in Fig. 2.1, but, it is equally valid to discuss the union of two **disjoint sets**. Typical disjoint sets are $C == \{1, 3, 5\}$ and $D == \{2, 4, 6\}$, which have no element in common and, for this reason, are said to be disjoint. In the case of these two sets, we have:

$C \cup D = \{1, 2, 3, 4, 5, 6\}$

The second operation on sets is known as **intersection** which, when it is applied to the two sets A and B given earlier in this section, returns a set which contains the elements that exist in both sets A and B. The intersection of A and B is written as $A \cap B$ so that

$A \cap B = \{6, 8\}$

In some cases two sets may have no elements in common. For instance, the intersection of the two sets C and D already given above is such that $C \cap D = \emptyset$ because both C and D have no elements in common. The concept of the intersection of two sets can usefully be illustrated using Venn diagrams as shown below:

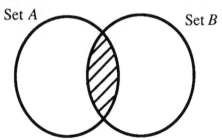

Set A   Set B

Fig. 2.2   The shaded area represents the
intersection of the two sets

which shows quite clearly that the intersection of two sets can be thought of as the region in common between them.

Another operation we consider is that of **set difference** which is widely used in **Z** specifications. The set difference of two sets, A and B, is denoted by $A \setminus B$ which is a set formed by removing from A the elements which occur both in A and B. Once again we will illustrate the concept prior to making a formal definition in section 2.9.

Taking set $A == \{2, 4, 6, 8\}$ and $B == \{1, 3, 5, 6, 7, 8, 9\}$, we find that the set difference $A \setminus B = \{2, 4\}$. $A \setminus B$ is shown pictorially on the Venn diagram below:

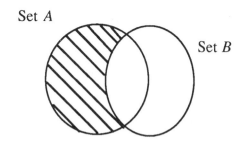

Fig. 2.3   The shaded area represents $A \setminus B$

2.7 Generalised union and intersection

The concept of the union of two sets can be extended to any number of sets. In this case, the union operator already defined acts on a set of sets. This generalised operator is distinguished from its binary equivalent, which acts on two sets, by an increase in size and is placed before the set on which it operates. For example, we have

$$\bigcup \{\{1, 2, 3\}, \{1, 4\}, \{1, 3\}\} = \{1, 2, 3, 4\}$$

The generalised intersection operator is defined in a similar manner. Again, it is an operator which is placed immediately before the set on which it operates. As an illustrative example, we have

$$\bigcap \{\{1, 2, 3\}, \{1, 4\}, \{1, 3\}\} = \{1\}$$

In each case we note that the generalised union and intersection operators act distributively across all members of the set on which they operate and, for this reason, they are sometimes referred to as the distributed union and intersection operator respectively.

Exercise 1
State the truth value - **false** or **true**- of the following:

(1) $\{1, 2\} \subset \{1, 2\}$ (2) $\{1, 2\} \subseteq \{1, 2\}$
(3) $1 \in \{1, 2\}$ (4) $1 \notin \{1, 2\}$

Given the sets A, B and C such that $A == \{1, 2, 3, 4\}$,
$B == \{2, 4, 6, 8, 10\}$ and $C == \{2, 3, 5, 7\}$ work out the following:

(5) $A \cup B$ (6) $A \cap B$ (7) $A \cup (B \cap C)$
(8) $A \cap (B \cup C)$ (9) $\bigcup \{A, B, C\}$ (10) $\bigcap \{A, B, C\}$
(11) $A \setminus B$ (12) $A \setminus (B \cap C)$

2.8 Set comprehension

The sets that we have discussed so far have all been defined by
enumeration e.g. $A == \{1, 2, 3\}$. An advantage of this approach is that
it reveals the elements that are contained in the set. However, one
disadvantage of this method is that if the set contains a lot of elements it
is tedious to write them all out and, in the case of infinite sets,
impossible. An alternative way of defining sets is by using set
comprehension. For example, if we wish to form a set, N_1, consisting
of all the positive integers greater than zero the definition by
enumeration would be:

$$N_1 == \{1, 2, 3, 4, 5, ...\}$$

This method is not entirely satisfactory in the case of infinite sets as we
have to be certain that sufficient elements are given in order that an
ambiguous interpretation of the set cannot be made. Using set
comprehension, we can write precisely:

$$N_1 == \{x : N \mid x > 0\}$$

where the vertical bar, '$\mid$', is read as 'such that' and where $x : N$ states
that the values of x will be drawn from the set, N, of natural numbers.
As we shall see, the statement $x : N$ is technically known as a type
declaration. The interpretation of this definition is that the set, N_1,
consists of all values of x greater than zero which is written in
mathematics as the inequality $x > 0$, where the symbol, $>$, means
literally 'greater than'. The condition after the vertical bar, involving the
variable x, is an example of what is technically called a **predicate** to
which can be attached one of two truth values - either it is **true** or
false.

As a further example of the usefulness of set comprehension, we
consider the set C of even numbers defined by enumeration as:

$C == \{2, 4, 6, 8, ... \}$

However, using set comprehension, we can write precisely:

$C == \{x : \mathbb{N} \mid x > 0 \bullet 2x \}$

where the 'bullet' $\bullet$, acts as another separator in this particular form of set comprehension. This example of set comprehension is the most general form as it allows for the optional inclusion of a 'term' after the bullet which will determine the values to be placed in the set C. However, in cases where the bullet is omitted as in the definition of $\mathbb{N}_1$, the values that are placed in the set are given by whatever occurs in the type declaration.

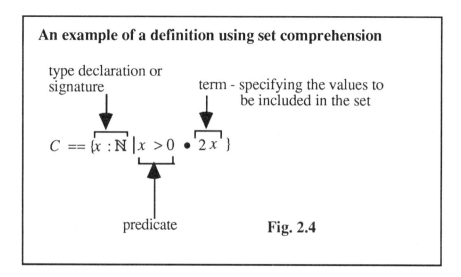

This definition can be illustrated more clearly in the definition box Fig. 2.4 in which the definition of set C falls into three parts. Firstly, we have a type declaration in which we state that each element, x, will be drawn from the set $\mathbb{N}$. Secondly, we state that each such element drawn from the set $\mathbb{N}$ will be passed through a predicate which acts as a filter and which only selects elements which return **true**. The third part, which occurs after the separating 'bullet' $\bullet$, simply states that the set C will consist of those x values drawn from $\mathbb{N}$ which also satisfy the predicate and which take the form given by the term. This example shows that set comprehension is also a useful technique for defining additional sets from sets that have already been given.

Example 1
Using set comprehension define a set, D, consisting of integers greater than 1 and which takes values $2x + 1$ where x is any natural number.

Solution
Step 1. To build this infinite set we need to take numbers from the set $\mathbb{N}$. Hence we must start with a type declaration $x : \mathbb{N}$ which says that all values of x will be drawn from the set $\mathbb{N}$.

Step 2. The members of the set D must be constructed from the members of the set $\mathbb{N}$. However, in order to select values greater than 1 to be placed in D, we require a predicate, $x > 0$, to act as a filter since we observe that when $x = 0$, the expression $2x + 1$ evaluates to 1.

Step 3. Finally, the members of the set D will be the values of $2x + 1$.

These three steps form the 'building blocks' of the set comprehension definition of the set D which is given by:

$$D == \{x : \mathbb{N} \mid x > 0 \bullet 2x + 1\}$$

To illustrate the actual values that go into the set and by way of contrast, the definition of the set D by enumeration would be:

$$D == \{3, 5, 7, 9, ...\}$$

We can now generalise these definitions to provide 'templates' to which all set comprehension definitions must conform. There are two cases to consider:

(1) where there is no term occurring after the bullet
(2) where there is a term occurring after the bullet, determining what goes into the set.

Case (1) is the simplest so we consider that first. The template for all such definitions takes the form:

Set comprehension without a term

type declaration

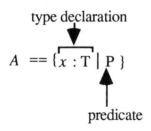

$$A \ == \{x : T \mid P \}$$

predicate

The contents of set A are those elements of type T which satisfy the predicate P

Fig. 2.5

The definition of the set $\mathbb{N}_1$ at the beginning of this section was an example of this sort of set comprehension.

In case (2) we allow the possibility that what goes into the set is determined by those elements of type T which satisfy the predicate and the resulting values of the term occurring after the bullet determine what is passed into the set. The template for such definitions takes the form:

Set comprehension with a term

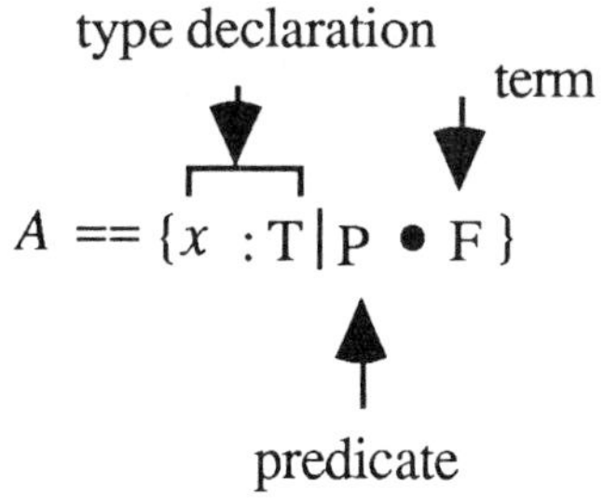

type declaration   term

$$A \ == \{x : T \mid P \bullet F \}$$

predicate

The elements of set A are determined by the term F

Fig. 2.6

An example of this sort of set comprehension definition is the set C given in Fig. 2.4 earlier.

2.9 Formal definitions of the set operators

Now that we have covered the concept of set comprehension, we can return to the set operators that we introduced earlier on with a view to presenting their formal definitions. It must be borne in mind that within the context of typed set theory these operators only work on sets containing elements of the same type which we will denote by T.

Formally, we can define the intersection of two sets C and D whose elements are of the same type T, in the following way:

$$C \cap D = \{x : T \mid x \in C \land x \in D\}$$

where the expression after the vertical bar, $|$, is a **compound predicate**. The particular predicate given above is a **conjunction** formed by means of the operator $\land$ which 'bolts' together two conditions. It takes the truth value of the first condition together with the truth value of the second and only returns **true** if they are both **true**. The first condition states that x must be a member of set C and the second condition states that x must also be a member of set D. The result is that the intersection of C and D contains elements in common to both of them.

We also informally considered the set union operator. If both A and B have the same type T, we can write formally:

$$A \cup B = \{x : T \mid x \in A \lor x \in B\}$$

where both A and B contain elements of the same type T and the **disjunction** operator, $\lor$, returns a **true** value if either of the propositions in the disjunction is **true**. It implies that the elements belong either to A or B or both simultaneously. The signature declaration in this definition ensures that the elements are drawn from sets of the same type. We can also see from this definition that the set union operator combines or joins together two sets of the same type.

The formal definition of the set difference, $D \setminus E$, is given by

$$D \setminus E = \{x : T \mid x \in D \land x \notin E\}$$

where both D and E are sets containing elements of the same type T. This definition states that the set difference of D and E will contain only those elements which are in D and not in E.

2.10 The cardinality of sets

The concept of size is an important feature of mathematics. In geometry, for example, the 'size' of a straight line used in constructing a regular polygon is given by its length. The corresponding concept in set theory is **cardinality**. The cardinality of a set is the number of unique elements in it and this provides a measure of its size.

For example, if we consider two sets A and B, given by:

$A == \{1, 2\}$
$B == \{3, 4, 5\}$

it is obvious that $A \neq B$. There is, however, another difference apart from the obvious one that the elements of A are not the same as those of B. It is simply that B contains more elements than A. In set terms, this means that the cardinality of B is greater than that of A.

The standard symbol in **Z** for the cardinality of a set is the hash symbol, #. This can be regarded as an operator which, when it is placed at the front of a set, returns the number of elements in the set. Hence, $\#B$ means the cardinality of set B. Using the cardinality operator, the statement that the cardinality of B is greater than that of A can be written as $\#B > \#A$ where, in this case, $\#B = 3$ and $\#A = 2$.

2.11 Power sets

For the purposes of illustration consider a set $A == \{1, 2\}$ containing just two elements. This set has the following proper subsets

$\{1\} \subset \{1, 2\}$

$\{2\} \subset \{1, 2\}$

The empty set, $\emptyset$, is a subset of every set. Hence we also have

$\emptyset \subset \{1, 2\}$

Moreover, every set is also a subset of itself so that we can also write

$\{1, 2\} \subseteq \{1, 2\}$

Using these subsets we can specify a new set called the **power set** of A, which will have as its elements all the subsets of A. Such a set is usually denoted by $\mathbb{P}A$ to denote that it is the power set derived from the set A. In this example we have

$\mathbb{P}\{1, 2\} == \{\emptyset, \{1\}, \{2\}, \{1, 2\}\}.$

We observe that $\{1\} \subseteq \{1, 2\}$ and also $\{1\} \subseteq \mathbb{P}\{1, 2\}$.

In general, we can formally write

$B \in \mathbb{P}A \Leftrightarrow B \subseteq A$

where the symbol, $\Leftrightarrow$, is a logical connective which will be dealt with in greater depth later, but, meanwhile we can interpret it as meaning 'equivalent'. In this definition it must be remembered that both A and B are sets and $\mathbb{P}A$ is a set of sets.

It can be shown that in general the power set of a set A of n elements has 2^n elements. Using the cardinality operator for sets, if $\#A = n$ then $\#\mathbb{P}A = 2^n$.

From the result above we can see that the cardinality of $\mathbb{P}A$ is finite if A itself is a finite set. However, if A is infinite, then $\mathbb{P}A$ is infinite. In **Z** it is usual to distinguish between these two possibilities by using the notation $\mathbb{F}A$ to denote the power set consisting of all finite subsets of A and reserving the notation $\mathbb{P}A$ to denote the set of all subsets of A. From these definitions we deduce that

$\mathbb{F}A \subseteq \mathbb{P}A$

We note that in general, given a type T the power set $\mathbb{P}T$ is again a type e.g. if $T = \mathbb{N}$ then $\mathbb{P}\mathbb{N}$ is the set consisting of all the sets of natural numbers. In connection with the underlying types of **Z**, we note that the statement $x : \mathbb{P}\mathbb{N}$ means that x is contained in $\mathbb{P}\mathbb{N}$. In general, however, given a generic type T, $\mathbb{F}T$ is not a type, since in this case $\mathbb{F}T \subseteq \mathbb{P}T$. Declarations of the form:

$x : \mathbb{F}T$

are abbreviations, since $\mathbb{F}T$ is itself a subset of $\mathbb{P}T$ and what is implied by this statement is that $x : \mathbb{P}T$.

As we shall see in subsequent chapters, the concept of a power set is particularly important in **Z**.

2.12 The Cartesian product of sets

We will now introduce the Cartesian product of two sets X and Y, written as $X \times Y$, which is defined as a new set containing pairs of elements each pair consisting of an element from set X followed by one from set Y. Before formally specifying the Cartesian product, we consider for illustrative purposes two sets X and Y given by:

$X == \{1, 2\}$ and $Y == \{3, 4\}$

Selecting an element from X and an element from Y, we can form what is called an **ordered pair**. Conventionally, the elements of an ordered pair are placed in round brackets and separated by a comma. As a typical example, we can form the ordered pair $(1, 3)$ from the sets X and Y by selecting the first element of X and the first element of Y. The set of all such ordered pairs constitutes the Cartesian product, $X \times Y$, of these two sets and is given by:

$X \times Y = \{(1, 3), (1, 4), (2, 3), (2, 4)\}$

In general, given two sets M and N:

$M == \{m_1, m_2, m_3, m_4, ...m_p\}$ and $N == \{n_1, n_2, n_3, n_4, ...n_q\}$

we can formally define the Cartesian product of these two sets as:

$M \times N = \{(m_1, n_1), ...(m_1, n_q), (m_2, n_1) ...(m_2, n_q) ...(m_p, n_q)\}$

From this we can see that the cardinality of the product set, $M \times N$, is related to the cardinality of M and N by:

$\#(M \times N) = \#M \times \#N$

Returning to the two sets X and Y above, we note that $\#X = 2$ and also $\#Y = 2$ with the result that $\#X \times \#Y = 4$ in agreement with the general principle just stated.

The concept of a Cartesian product can be extended to any number of sets. For example, we can form the Cartesian product $X \times Y \times Z$ of sets X, Y and Z in which each element is a **tuple**, (x_i, y_j, z_k), consisting of one element from X, followed by one element from Y and terminating with an element from Z.

To illustrate this concept we define the set Z:

$Z == \{2, 5\}$

The Cartesian product, $X \times Y \times Z$, is then given by

$X \times Y \times Z = \{(1, 3, 2), (1, 4, 2), (2, 3, 2), (2, 4, 2), (1, 3, 5),$
$(1, 4, 5), (2, 3, 5), (2, 4, 5)\}$

Example 2
The IBM personal computer (PC) is capable of operating its screen in either text or graphics mode. Each mode is different from the other and they are mutually exclusive.

In order to show a practical application of the Cartesian product of sets, we consider the problem of identifying any pixel(point) on the VDU of a PC in graphical mode. The EGA graphics adaptor has a set of coordinates ranging from 0 to 639 horizontally, and 0 to 349 vertically with the origin of the system in the top left hand side corner as shown below:

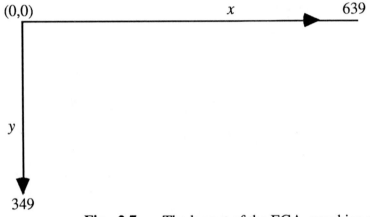

Fig. 2.7   The layout of the EGA graphics screen

Following the usual convention of labelling axes, we take x horizontal and y vertical but with the positive direction going downwards. A unique combination of (x, y) in the given range specifies a pixel on the VDU screen. In order to identify an individual pixel, we introduce the sets:

$X == \{x : \mathbb{N} \mid x < 640\}$ and $Y == \{y : \mathbb{N} \mid y < 350\}$

The set of all pixels is now given by $X \times Y$.

Example 3
In order to illustrate that the concept of a Cartesian product can be extended to any number of sets, we can develop the above example relating to the VDU graphics screen by associating a colour with each pixel. Each pixel now has 3 attributes:

    (1) an x coordinate such that $x \in X$

    (2) a y coordinate such that $y \in Y$

(3) a colour which is usually identified by an integer in the range 0..15.

The reader should note that the notation _.._ is used to represent number ranges. For example, 0..15 denotes a set containing the natural numbers in the range 0 up to 15 inclusive:

$$0..15 = \{0, 1, 2, 3, 4, 5, 6, 7, 8, 9, 10, 11, 12, 13, 14, 15\}$$

These colour codes are all members of the set which can be defined using set comprehension as *Colour* == $\{c : \mathbb{N} \mid c < 16\}$.

Each pixel is a member of the Cartesian product $X \times Y \times Colour$.

2.13 Summary

In this chapter we have formally introduced the concept of a typed set which is used extensively in **Z**. Moreover, we have looked at the operations that can be performed on sets and these concepts will be used extensively in the following chapters as our understanding of **Z** unfolds and develops.

The concept of a typed set is fundamental to much of the way in which we organise information in everyday life e.g. a set of telephone numbers, a set of cars. It is for this reason that sets provide the mathematical underpinning to the specification language **Z**, which is primarily concerned with capturing and modelling system requirements.

Exercise 2
Given the sets A, B and C such that $A == \{1, 2, 3, 4\}$, $B == \{2, 4, 6, 8, 10\}$ and $C == \{2, 3, 5, 7\}$ work out the following:

(1) $\mathbb{P}C$ (2) $A \times C$ (3) #B (4) #A
(5) #($A \times B$)

Write down the elements in the sets defined below:

(6) $\{x : \mathbb{N} \mid x < 10 \bullet x^2\}$
(7) $\{x : \mathbb{N}_1 \mid x < 5 \bullet 1/x\}$

Using set comprehension define the following sets:

(8) A set *Odds* consisting of all odd, integer numbers < 20.
(9) A set *Evens* consisting of all the even, integer numbers < 20.
(10) A set *PerfectSquares* consisting of perfect squares in the range 1 up to 100 inclusive.

3

Functions

3.1 Introduction

In chapter 2 we studied the way objects can be organised and defined using sets. In this chapter and the next, we will look at the links between sets of different objects. These links are classified as **functions** and **relations**. We will consider functions first, although as we shall see in chapter 4, a function is a special case of a relation. In order to represent functions, standard mathematical notation is used as well as special **Z** notation. Where the **Z** notation differs this will be emphasised in the text.

At the end of this chapter the reader should:

♦ understand the basic concepts of functions

♦ be able to define and classify different types of functions

♦ understand the application of the different concepts of functions to simple models

♦ be able to formalise the use of functions in simple specifications

3.2 Functions

In everyday life we use the terms function and functional to convey ideas about the use and usefulness of objects, machines and people. It is common in business parlance to talk about functional relations. For example, a personnel department may be responsible for recruitment and this may be described as 'recruitment being a function of personnel'. However, in formal methods in order for the term function to be effective, it must be clearly defined and unambiguously understood.

When we examine the recruitment function more closely we see that this has an output in the form of additional staff and we know that the personnel department performs the action which produces this result. There are many other examples of functions in computing. Any user of a microcomputer soon becomes familiar with the special keys called function keys, which each carry out one specific operation. For example, the F3 function key, on most personal computers, will re-echo the last command entered into the keyboard. In spreadsheets too, we commonly use built-in functions to carry out specific actions such as $SUM(a_1..a_{10})$ where SUM is a function which will add a list of numbers in a row or a column. We expect such a function to give a simple, predictable and reliable output from a suitable input. If the input is inappropriate for the function, the output is an error. For example, if we use $SUM(a_1..a_{10})$ for a column containing string values, then an error message will be displayed. To summarise, in real world examples a function carries out a transformation of an input into an output in a predictable way.

In formal methods the objective is to use the concept of a function to model real world relationships. In this context, a function is a way of describing a specific link or **mapping** between two sets. It means that one member of the first set can map to only one member of the second set. In a systems specification, this link can be called a functional relationship or functional dependency since the value of the member of the second set in the mapping depends only upon the value of the member of the first set.

We will now look at a simple numerical example of a function before we consider the kinds of functions we may meet in systems specifications. Fig. 3.1 below considers the *square* function in this way acting on the sets indicated in the diagram.

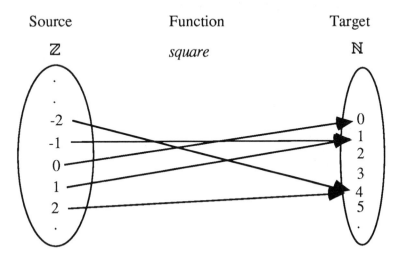

Fig. 3.1   A function as a mapping

This example is consistent with our initial ideas of a function since, when we square any element in the domain, one and only one, element in the target set is obtained. The *square* function is reliable and predictable. In our example the *square* function accepts any member from the source $\mathbb{Z}$ and returns a member of the target set $\mathbb{N}$. This simple example shows the main features needed for a formal definition of a function. The function accepts a member from a defined set and produces a unique result which is a member of another defined set.

Returning to our example of the specification of a personnel system, the recruitment function accepts a member of the set of applicants and produces an additional member of the set of staff. In developing a specification for a system in **Z**, it is essential to identify all the functional relationships between the sets of interest. Here are some examples of functional relationships found in computer systems:

> in a payroll system , employees map to job title
> in a stock control system, products map to price
> in a transportation system, vehicle maps to driver
> in a service system, contract maps to customer

3.3 The formal definition of functions

Functions are used in many applications in programming languages, databases and spreadsheets. Since functions are so widely used, a number of different methods of defining them have developed.

We can define a function f as a specific mapping from set A to set B such that every member of the set A corresponds to one and only one member of the set B. This can be shown by the use of an arrow from set A to set B as follows:

$$f : A \rightarrow B$$

The notation $A \rightarrow B$ represents the set of all the possible functions from A to B. Any particular function will be a subset of the Cartesian product $\mathbb{P}(A \times B)$. In **Z** the type of any function f between two sets A and B will be the Cartesian product $\mathbb{P}(A \times B)$, even though a particular function may be a subset of the Cartesian product. However, in writing function declarations in **Z** schemas, it is common practice to use either $\mathbb{P}(A \times B)$ or $A \rightarrow B$. The use of the functional mapping arrow $A \rightarrow B$ can be more informative in declarations as it gives more detail about the relationship.

Since a function is a set, it can be defined in the same way as a set, either by set comprehension or by enumeration. The particular function *square* can be described by enumeration as follows:

$$square == \{..., (1, 1), (2, 4), (3, 9), (4, 16), ...\}$$

As we have seen in chapter 2, the definition of functions by set comprehension involves the use of predicates to describe the way the elements of the range can be obtained from the domain. We will introduce some functions in this way now but this topic is covered in greater detail in chapter 8.

The notation $A \rightarrow B$ means that a function is a set defined as a mapping from A to B. Another technical way of describing a function is to say b is the **image** of a or $b = f\, a$. The value a upon which the image b depends is called the **argument**. If $a \in A$ and $b \in B$ such that $f\, a = b$ we can say that $(a, b) \in f$ and regard (a, b) as an ordered pair. The ordered pair describes the functional mapping by listing the argument, followed by its image. In mathematics and in many programming languages the argument of a function is given in brackets after the function name so that we write $f(a) = b$. In **Z** the brackets need not be used. The range is therefore the set of all the possible images from the function f.

The set of all the arguments upon which the image depends is called the **domain** of the function. The domain of the function is always shown on the left in a mapping diagram and may be a subset of the source. The output set which contains the results is known as the **target** and is shown on the right in a mapping diagram, while the set of images which is a subset of the target, is known as the **range** of the function. In Fig. 3.1 the domain is identical to the source, the set **Z** , and the target is the set **N**.

When we consider the *square* function again in Fig. 3.2 below, we see that although 2, 3 and 5 appear in the target they do not appear in the range because they are not squares of natural numbers.

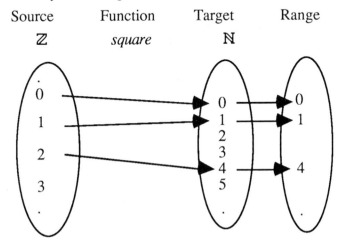

Fig. 3.2   source, target and range

Z uses two special functions called **dom** and **ran** to give the domain and range sets of any function. Using dom *square* and ran *square* to denote the domain and range respectively of *square*, we can summarise these important results as follows:

$$\text{dom } square = \mathbb{Z} \text{ and ran } square \subset \mathbb{N}$$

where ran *square* consists of the squares of all the natural numbers and can be defined by enumeration as:

$$\text{ran } square = \{0, 1, 4, 9, 16, 25, ...\}$$

In the case of this example the source and the domain of the function *square* are identical, while the range is a subset of the target.

An alternative method of writing the ordered pair (a, b) is by using the maplet notation $a \mapsto b$, in which we think of a being mapped to b. Hence, a set S consisting of the following ordered pairs

$$S == \{(1, 2), (3, 6), (4, 5)\}$$

can be written in maplet notation as

$$S == \{1 \mapsto 2, 3 \mapsto 6, 4 \mapsto 5\}$$

We will now illustrate these concepts in the following two examples.

Example 1
The first example considers the formal definition of a function called *absquare* which maps elements of the domain $\mathbb{N}$ to its corresponding squared value in the target $\mathbb{N}$.

We can define the function *absquare* using set comprehension:

$$absquare == \{n : \mathbb{N} \bullet n \mapsto n^2\}$$

The mappings can be given in the $\mathbb{Z}$ format of argument and image as follows:

$$absquare\ 1 = 1 \quad absquare\ 2 = 4 \quad\quad absquare\ 3 = 9 \quad\quad absquare\ 4 = 16$$

An alternative method of showing the relationship between an argument and its image is by enclosing the argument in brackets:

$$absquare(3) = 9$$

Since $\mathbb{N}$ is the domain and the range is the set $\{0, 1, 4, 9, 16, 25, ...\}$ we can write:

dom *absquare* = N
ran *absquare* = {0, 1, 4, 9, 16, 25, ...}

All the information above could be set out in a Z schema called *square_op* in the following style:

```
┌── square_op ──────────
│ n : N
│ absquare : N → N
├──────────────────────
│ absquare n = n²
└──────────────────────
```

Fig. 3.3 A schema function

The declaration in the top section of the schema box is called the signature of the function. In the lower part of the schema we can add any detail we wish in the form of predicates to complete the specification.

Example 2
Readers familiar with programming languages can recognise that the concept of a function as a mapping between sets is implicitly used. The following example from Pascal illustrates the point:

```
TYPE
    domain = 1..5;
    target = 1..30;
FUNCTION  square(invalue:domain):target;
BEGIN
        square:= invalue*invalue
END;
```

The square function created by this fragment of code uses invalue as the parameter of the function. When we use the square function in, for example, a statement such as square(2), the 2 passed to the function is the argument and the result must be a value contained in the target.

In examples 1 and 2 we have considered two very simple functions in detail. However, the domain of a function need not be a simple set, it could itself be a Cartesian product. The argument of such a function would be a tuple (see chapter 2, section 2.12) rather than a single value. This would be the way the SUM function in the spreadsheet example mentioned in section 3.2 would be mapped. Finally it is important to understand that in Z, functions are regarded as static mappings between the domain and the range and nothing is implied about the methods or algorithms which might be used to obtain the result.

3.4 The λ-notation (Lambda abstraction)

In **Z** it is possible to use λ-**notation** as a shorthand notation for
defining functions by set comprehension. For example, instead of
defining the *absquare* function as we have above, with λ-notation it
may be defined as:

$$absquare == \lambda a : \mathbb{N} \ \bullet \ a * a$$

This short cut uses declarations to fix the domain and this is followed
by an expression for the typical range element rather than by using a
mapping notation. The bullet • separates the declaration from the
expression giving the range element.

In general the format followed is λD | P • E where D represents
declarations, E expressions and P optional predicate constraints. In the
example just given there are no constraints so the constraint bar has
been omitted, but an example where it has been included is given later.
This notation will be used in **Z** specifications in later chapters.

3.5 Different kinds of functions

A number of different kinds of functions exist and when using them in
formal specifications it is helpful to recognise these differences and their
consequences. For the *square* function every member of the domain $\mathbb{Z}$
will give an acceptable or defined output. This sort of function is called
a **total function** and this is indicated by the particular arrow drawn
from *A* to *B* as shown below:

$$f : A \ \rightarrow \ B$$

We use the letter *f* for the function but by mathematical convention we
could use any other lower case letter from *f* to *m*. However in a **Z**
specification it is more usual to use a short meaningful name. Not all
functions are total functions, since many real life examples cannot be
defined for the whole of the domain. In this case the function is called a
partial function and this is indicated by a different arrow:

$$f : A \ \nrightarrow \ B$$

representing the set of partial functions from *A* to *B* of type $\mathbb{P}(A \times B)$.

In the personnel recruitment function the type of the function *recruit* is
$\mathbb{P}$ (*Applicants* × *Staff*). The domain is the set of *Applicants* to the
company. Some applicants are recruited and are included in the set
Staff. Those that are not recruited obviously are not members of the
Staff set. The recruitment function is a partial function because the fate

of the applicants who do not become staff members is not defined.

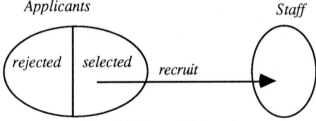

Fig. 3.4 A partial function

rejected $\cup$ selected = Applicants
rejected $\cap$ selected = Ø
recruit : Applicants $\nrightarrow$ Staff

In many database applications it is important to recognise the difference between partial and total functions. Interrogations using partial functions will not always produce a result since they may generate the empty set or a null result. We can specify a total function as a partial function where the domain is the whole of the source. The type declaration of all total functions from A to B is defined as

$$A \rightarrow B == \{f : A \nrightarrow B \mid \text{dom} f = A\}$$

In a music library system we may want to keep records about popular artists and may use a function which maps the artists to their sex.

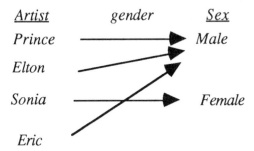

In this case the *gender* function is a total function as the domain is the whole of the source. It is also a function where the range is the whole of the target set. This is called a **surjective function**. Surjective functions are also known as **onto** functions and are shown by the use of a special double-headed arrow as follows:

$$f : A \twoheadrightarrow B$$

The definition of a surjective function can be given in terms of a partial function as

$A \twoheadrightarrow B == \{f : A \twoheadrightarrow B \mid \operatorname{ran} f = B\}$

The *gender* function is a total function and should give a non-empty response from the database for every artist's name.

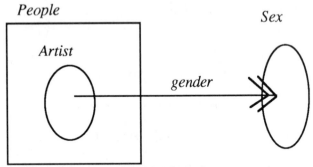

Fig. 3.5 A surjective function

gender is a total surjective function as it maps the whole of the domain to the whole of the target. In this example, we have:

$$\text{dom } gender = Artist$$
$$gender : Artist \twoheadrightarrow Sex$$

In contrast the *absquare* function is a case where the target does not equal the range and it is not therefore a **surjective** function. There are other differences about the *absquare* and *gender* functions. For example, each member of the domain in *absquare* maps to a different member of the range. This is known as a **one-to-one function**. In the case of the *gender* function, many artists map to *Male*, many to *Female*, so this is not a one-to-one function.

One-to-one functions are known as **injective** functions. A function given by:

$f : A \rightarrow B$

is said to be injective or one-to-one if no two elements of the domain A map to the same element of the range, B. An injective function is shown by the use of a special arrow:

$f : A \rightarrowtail B$

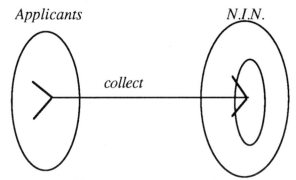

Fig. 3.6 An injective function

In the personnel system it may be necessary to collect the National Insurance Numbers (N.I.N) of the job applicants. Every applicant will have a unique National Insurance Number and the function *collect* will be an injective function. It is not surjective as there will be other N.I.N.'s which do not correspond to applicants. In this example:

ran *collect* $\subseteq$ *N.I.N* and dom *collect* = *Applicants*

Fig. 3.7 presents a comparison of the different mapping diagrams of these types of functions:

f_1 is a surjective function as every element of the target is generated by the function

f_2 is an injective or one-to-one function since each value of the domain maps to a different value but because there is no value of x corresponding to any element in the domain, the range of f_2 is not equal to the target and it is not surjective

f_3 is both injective and surjective and is called a **bijective function** or a **one-to-one correspondence**

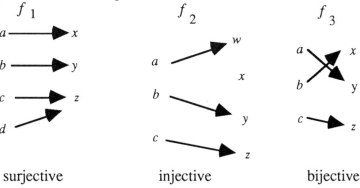

Fig. 3.7   Different kinds of functions

f_3 is a bijection and would be indicated by the use of a further arrow as follows:

$$f_3 : A \rightarrowtail\!\!\!\rightarrow B$$

and can be defined as

$$A \rightarrowtail\!\!\!\rightarrow B == (A \rightarrow\!\!\!\rightarrow B) \cap (A \rightarrowtail B)$$

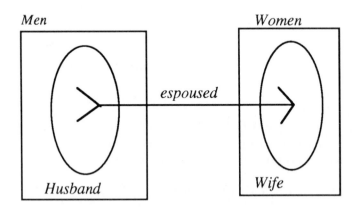

Men   *Women*

espoused

Husband   *Wife*

Fig. 3.8 A bijective function

As an example of a bijective function, we consider the function *espoused* between husbands and wives. This function is bijective since every wife is mapped to a husband and *vice versa*. In this example

dom *espoused* = *Husband*
ran *espoused* = *Wife*

Surjective and injective functions can be partial or total functions. However a bijective function maps the elements of the domain to the elements of the range by a one-to-one correspondence and cannot be a partial function.

In writing **Z** specifications it is important not only to identify the functional relationships operating in a particular system but to be able to classify the functions into their different kinds. This can add a great deal of detail to a specification which may be vital in the case of safety critical systems. When we identify a bijective function in a specification we will know that every member of both sets will be involved in the mapping and there will be no 'loose ends'.

Summary

Total Function	$f : A \to B$
Partial function	$f : A \nrightarrow B$
Injective function(one-to-one)	$f : A \rightarrowtail B$
Partial injective function	$f : A \nrightarrowtail B$
Surjective function(onto)	$f : A \twoheadrightarrow B$
Partial surjective function	$f : A \twoheadleftarrow B$
Bijective function(one-to-one correspondence)	$f : A \rightarrowtail\!\!\!\to B$

We are now going to illustrate these different functions with some simple numerical examples before we consider the kind of functions met in specifications.

Example 3

Consider the simple function $f(x) = x + 1$ where $f : \mathbb{N} \to \mathbb{N}_1$. The function can be declared in lambda notation as

$$\lambda x : \mathbb{N}, y : \mathbb{N}_1 \mid y = x + 1 \bullet y$$

In this example, there is a constraint, $y = x + 1$, hence the constraint bar is required. The function produces the following results:

$$f\ 0 = 1, f\ 1 = 2, f\ 2 = 3$$

We can see that there is a unique image from the function corresponding to each argument. Thus the function is injective. In the same way we can see that for any element of the target it is possible to find a corresponding value of the domain which will satisfy the function. The function is therefore surjective. The function is both surjective and injective and consequently it is a bijection so that

$$f : \mathbb{N} \rightarrowtail\!\!\!\to \mathbb{N}_1$$

Example 4

Let A denote the set of natural numbers $\{1, 2, 3, 4\}$ and B the set consisting of $\{1, 2, 3\}$. The surjective function, $f : A \twoheadrightarrow B$, in this case is $f(n) = \lfloor n/2 \rfloor + 1$. Here $\lfloor x \rfloor$ represents the floor or the largest integer less than or equal to x. For example, $\lfloor 2.4 \rfloor = 2$ and $\lfloor 3.7 \rfloor = 3$.

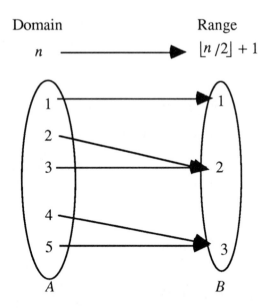

Domain

$n \xrightarrow{\hspace{3cm}} \lfloor n /2 \rfloor + 1$

Range

We see that there will always be at least one element of *A* mapping to each element of *B*. This function is surjective but it is not injective as it is not a one-to-one function.

3.6 Inverse functions

In many systems specifications we will be interested in both directions of the link between the sets involved. In the previous section we considered the function *recruit* which mapped *Applicants* to *Staff*. If the organisation is interested in information about the way its selection policy is operating, for example to check for any kind of discrimination, the mapping between *Staff* and *Applicants* may be important as well. This function which we can call *select* will be the **inverse** of the *recruit* function.

$$recruit : Applicants \to Staff$$
$$select : Staff \to Applicants$$

However, we need to be sure that when we reverse the sets in a functional relationship, the resulting link is still a function. We can reverse the effects of the *absquare* function in example 1 of section 3.3 because it is an injective or one-to-one function. The reverse operation we will call *abroot*. The function *abroot* will be a partial function since *absquare* is not a surjective function. We can write

$$abroot : \mathbb{N} \nrightarrow \mathbb{N}$$

abroot is the **inverse** of function *absquare*. In the same way *absquare* is the inverse function of *abroot*. In general if f is an injective function such that $f : A \twoheadrightarrow B$, then f^{-1} denotes the inverse of f and is given by:

$$f^{-1} : B \to A$$

f^{-1} is a unique function such that $\operatorname{dom} f^{-1} = \operatorname{ran} f$.

Example 5

For the purposes of illustration, we will consider a function f and its inverse f^{-1}, each linking together two sets A and B in a complementary manner.

$$f : A \to B \qquad\qquad f : \{(a, s), (b, t), (c, r)\}$$

$$A == \{a, b, c\} \qquad\qquad B == \{r, s, t\}$$

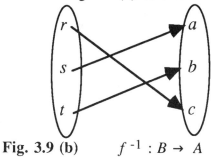

Fig. 3.9 (a) $f : A \to B$

The inverse function $f^{-1} = \{(s, a), (t, b), (r, c)\}$ is a function from B to A. The mapping is shown in Fig. 3.9 (b) below.

Fig. 3.9 (b) $f^{-1} : B \to A$

There are many examples of inverse functions which are used in mathematics. For example, $\cos \theta$ and $\cos^{-1} \theta$ are inverse functions of each other. In contrast the *gender* function cannot be switched over in this way because each member of the range maps to many members of the *artists* set. The *gender* function does not therefore have an inverse function. Injections are functions whose inverses are also functions.

Example 6
Consider a vending machine which offers the following selections:

Drinks	Price
Orange	25
Coffee	30
Cola	20
Tea	15

The domain is the set *Drinks* == {*Orange*, Coffee, *Cola, Tea*}. The target *Price* can be taken as $\mathbb{N}$, the natural numbers. The function from *Drinks* to *Price* is a total function, as the domain of the function is the set of *Drinks*. It is a one-to-one function or an injection since every drink has a different price, but it is not a surjection.

$$f: Drinks \rightarrowtail \mathbb{N}$$

The inverse function, however, is a partial function because the domain is not the whole of the set *Price*. It is, however, a surjection as the target equals the range.

$$f^{-1}: \mathbb{N} \twoheadrightarrow Drinks$$

Example 7
Functions are provided in many programming languages to convert alpha-numeric characters into the corresponding ASCII codes. Fig. 3.10 represents such a pair of inverse functions, one of which *Code* gives the decimal code when the input is the normal ASCII character set and the other *Char* gives the character when the ASCII code is input.

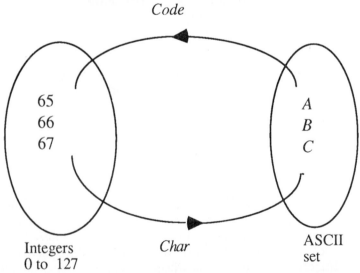

Fig. 3.10   Inverse Functions

In Fig. 3.10 the domain of *Char* is exactly the range of *Code* and vice versa. Both functions are injective and we have $Char^{-1}C = Code\ C = 67$ as a typical result.

Exercise 1
(1) Given the following functions *f, g, h* such that
f = {(4, 2), (7, 6), (2, 7), (9, 8)}, $g\ x = 2^x$ with domain 0..5 and
$h\ x = x^2$ with the domain 0..3:

(a) find the range of each function
(b) which of the above functions are injective ?
(c) which of the above functions have inverses ?
(d) give the domain and range of each inverse function.

(2) Given *M* is the set of married men, *W* the set of married women we can define the following functions:
$f\ x$ = wife of *x* where $f : M \rightarrow W$,
$g\ x$ = husband of *x* where $g : W \rightarrow M$

Assuming no bigamy, are *f* and *g* inverse functions ?

3.7 Composition of functions

Suppose we have two functions, the first function *f* from set *A* to set *B* and the second function *g* from set *B* to set *C*. We can then define a new function from *A* to *C* which is called the **composition** of *f* with *g*. In mathematical texts composition is usually written *g o f*. However, in **Z** it is written *f ; g* to show a forward composition from *A* to *B* to *C*.

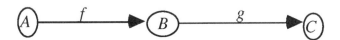

The composition of the function written as *g o f* or *f ; g* is the equivalent of following the arrows *f* and *g* in Fig. 3.11 below:

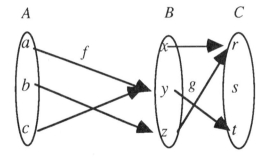

Fig. 3.11 The Composition of Functions

We can express Fig. 3.11 as a series of images from A to B to C using the composition operator as follows

$$g \text{ of } a = g(f(a)) = g \, y = t$$

The function f from A to B is composed with g the function from B to C. The image of the argument a in f is y. The image of the argument y in g is t. In the same way we can write:

$$g \text{ of } b = g(f(b)) = g \, z = r$$
$$g \text{ of } c = g(f(c)) = g \, y = t$$

For the composite function $g \text{ of }$ or $f \, \text{\textfrac} \, g$, the range of f must be the same set as the domain of g. Composite functions behave in such a way that if f and g are both injective then the composite function will also be injective. If both f and g are surjective then the composite function is also surjective.

We can formally define the domain of the composition $f \, \text{\textfrac} \, g$ for two functions $f : A \rightarrow B$ and $g : B \rightarrow C$ as the set:

$$\text{dom} f \text{\textfrac} \, g \; == \; \{x : A \mid x \in \text{dom} f \wedge fx \in \text{dom} g\}$$

3.8 Function overriding

In many computer applications where functions are used, the values returned by a function will need to be updated from time to time. For example, a function *pay* maps staff to a set of numbers. Let *Staff* be the set of staff members and *pay* a function which returns the hourly rate of pay of each member in pounds.

$pay = \{Mary \mapsto 10, John \mapsto 12, Jackie \mapsto 13, Paul \mapsto 8\}$

When the pay of any member of staff changes, it will be necessary to ensure that the function *pay* provides the correct answer. This can be achieved by using **function overriding** which is symbolised as $\oplus$. When *John's* hourly pay is reduced to 10 the operation of function overriding ensures the function will return the correct value i.e.

$pay \oplus \{John \mapsto 10\} = \{Mary \mapsto 10, John \mapsto 10, Jackie \mapsto 13, Paul \mapsto 8\}$

The overriding operator $\oplus$ combines two functions of the same type to give a new function. In the above example the first function is *pay* and the second function is a set containing a maplet for a single update of the data but any number of ordered pairs could be included. We can see that, for any two functions f and g of the same type, $f \oplus g$ is defined for any member x provided that x is a member of the domain of f or the domain of g. In a **Z** specification this means we can describe the situation of updating a file with a single record or through merging with another data file.

Formally, we can state that if $x \in$ dom g, then $(f \oplus g)x = g$. However, if $x \notin$ dom g but $x \in$ dom f, then $(f \oplus g)x = f x$. The notation $f \oplus g$ can be read as *f overriden by g*.

If the *pay* function above is overridden by another function called *update* which contains all the changes in the pay details we write:

newpay = pay $\oplus$ *update*

The domain of the *newpay* function is the result of the union of the domains of the separate functions so that

dom (*pay* $\oplus$ *update*) = (dom *pay*) $\cup$ (dom *update*)

If *update* contains only new pay details to be added, then:

(dom *pay*) $\cap$ (dom *update*) = $\varnothing$ and *pay* $\oplus$ *update* = *pay* $\cup$ *update*

3.9 Functions in an application

In this section we apply the concepts studied so far to the specification of part of an application.

Example 8
A music library keeps records of compact discs which can be borrowed. The records have the following structure:

Title	Artist	Songs	Style
Boomania	Betty Boo	11	Rap/Dance
Dreamland	Blackbox	7	Dance
Dangerous	Michael Jackson	14	Pop
Mind Adventures	Desree	10	Soul
On Every Street	Dire Straits	12	Rock
Bad	Michael Jackson	10	Pop

We will use this file to look at the functional relationships between the separate columns.

The reader should examine the data carefully to interpret the relationship between each pair of columns. Each column corresponds to a set in the domain of interest. We will call these sets *Title*, *Artist*, *Songs* and *Style*. The set *Title* contains all the titles of the compact discs in the library and the set *Artist* contains all the names of the artists. *Songs* is the number of songs on each compact disc. *Style* is the set of keywords decided by the users and is defined as:

Style == {*Rap/Dance, Pop, Dance, Soul, Rock*}

We now consider a number of functions, which can be derived from the above table.

a) $f : Title \twoheadrightarrow Artist$
This is a surjective function because the domain of *Title* maps to the whole of the target, the set *Artist*, but it is not injective as we can see that there are two titles assigned to Michael Jackson.

b) $g : Title \twoheadrightarrow Songs$
In this case *Songs* can be modelled from the set of natural numbers. The function from the set *Title* to *Songs* is then a function where the target does not equal the range as only numbers between 5 and 25 appear in the range. We can write

$Songs == \{n : \mathbb{N} \mid n > 5 \wedge n < 25 \bullet n\}$

This is an example of a function which is neither surjective nor injective.

c) $h : Artist \twoheadrightarrow Style$
This is a surjective function but it is not injective as more than one title corresponds to the same style.

d) $Artist \leftrightarrow Songs$
On examination this is not a function as it does not meet the criteria that one element of the domain maps to one element of the range. *Michael Jackson* from the set of artists maps to two values for songs, 14 and 10. *Artist* will still be defined as a set even if *Michael Jackson* is listed twice. This is just an example of redundancy.

e) The two functions *f* and *h* can be composed to give a function $f \, \S \, h$ which maps *Title* to *Style*, as below:

Title	Artist	Style
Boomania	Betty Boo	Rap/Dance
Dreamland	Blackbox	Dance
Dangerous	Michael Jackson	Pop
Mind Adventures	Desree	Soul
On Every Street	Dire Straits	Rock
Bad	Michael Jackson	

Then $f \, \S \, h \, (Bad) = Pop$ and $f \, \S \, h(Dangerous) = Pop$.

3.10 Summary

In this chapter the concept of a function has been introduced. Moreover, the various kinds of function have been defined and illustrated by a number of examples drawing on both finite and infinite sets.

We are now in a position to identify the main functions in a systems specification and to analyse the functional relationships in detail in order to classify the functions into the various kinds. At this point in the text it may be worthwhile pointing out there is a further classification that can be made of partial functions and partial injective functions into finite partial and finite partial injective functions but we defer a full discussion of this until chapter 8. Instead we have concentrated on capturing the correct functional correspondence between the sets under consideration.

The main keywords used in this chapter are summarised below:

FUNCTION   KEYWORDS

Function	$f : A \to B$
Source	A
Domain	$\subseteq A$
Target	B
Range(range is a proper subset of target)	$\subseteq B$
Total Function	$f : A \to B$
Partial function	$f : A \nrightarrow B$
Injective function(one-to-one)	$f : A \rightarrowtail B$
Surjective function(onto)	$f : A \twoheadrightarrow B$
Bijective function(one-to-one correspondence)	$f : A \rightarrowtail\!\!\!\!\to B$
Composition forward	$g \,\fatsemi\, f$
backward	$g \circ f$
Inverse function	f^{-1}
Function Overriding	$f \oplus g$

Exercise 2
(1) For the vending machine described in example 6 section 3.6, write formal expressions for the following:

(a) the price of *Cola* is increased to 35 p
(b) what will be the effect on the functions if the price of *Cola* is increased to 25 p?

(2) For the music library application, write formal expressions for:

(a) the addition of another CD title to the library
(b) changing the number of songs for *Dreamland* to 8

(3) Given the functions f and g defined by the following sets of ordered pairs:

$$f = \{(a, x), (b, y), (c, z)\}$$
$$g = \{(1, a), (2, a), (3, c)\}$$

(a) determine $g \, ; f$ as a set of ordered pairs
(b) if we define a new function, $h = g \, ; f$, does h^{-1} exist ?

(4) As we have seen in Example 1, schemas can be used to define functions. Write the schema block for *cube_op* using a function $cube(x) = x^3$ with a domain and range consisting of the real numbers.

(5) Write a schema, *Select*, which introduces a partial function and two variables as follows:

(a) a partial function, *Sieve*, which maps natural numbers into sets of natural numbers.

(b) the two variables, *MinSize* and *MaxSize*, both of type $\mathbb{N}$

The schema should include a predicate which states that *Select* will never map a natural number into a set whose cardinality is less than *MinSize* and greater than *MaxSize*.

4

Relations

4.1 Introduction

The previous chapter introduced the concept of a function as a special mapping between two sets. In this chapter we look at a more general connection between sets which is known as a **relation**. It is important that the differences between relations and functions are well understood and that they are used appropriately in preparing systems specifications.

At the end of this chapter the reader should:

♦ understand the basic concept of a relation

♦ be able to define and classify different types of relations

♦ understand that a function is a special type of relation

♦ be able to apply the concepts of relations in applications

4.2 Relations

When we looked at the music library file in section 3.9 of chapter 3 we found that the relationship between the sets *Artist* and *Songs* could not be modelled as a function since one artist mapped to more than one value. There are many real world relationships and patterns which fall into this category. Relations are a way of dealing with these problems. We meet relations in every day language. Consider a set of mothers M and their sons S and look at the relationship between them:

$$M == \{Diana, Anne\}$$
$$S == \{William, Harry, Peter\}$$

We want a formal way of describing which mother and son belong together. One way of modelling a relationship between two sets which we have already met in functions is through the Cartesian product introduced in section 2.12 of chapter 2. For example, the Cartesian product for the sets M and S would be:

$$M \times S = \{(Diana, William), (Diana, Harry), (Diana, Peter),$$
$$(Anne, William), (Anne, Harry), (Anne, Peter)\}$$

However we know that a son can only have one mother so that only a subset of the Cartesian product will describe this relation and we know that a mapping exists which links the mothers and their sons. Fig. 4.1 below shows *Diana* as the mother of *William* and *Harry*, while *Anne* is the mother of *Peter*. Then we can see that the relation consists of the following pairs {(*Diana, William*), (*Diana, Harry*), (*Anne, Peter*)}. These ordered pairs belong to the relation and the other pairs do not.

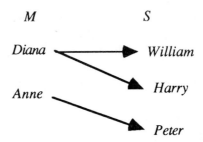

Fig. 4.1 A relational mapping

A relation can be regarded as dividing a Cartesian product into two disjoint subsets one of which is in the relation and the other is not. No ordered pair can belong to both subsets. There are many examples of numerical relations particularly for comparing numbers. The relational operators <, >, <=, >= all represent relations. For example, we can compare the elements of the two sets of numbers A and B below in Fig. 4.2.

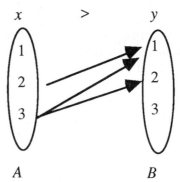

Fig. 4.2 'Greater than' as a relation

The relation $x > y$ where $x \in A$ and $y \in B$ consists of the pairs {(2, 1), (3, 2), (3, 1)} from the Cartesian product of A and B. Although the pairs {(1, 1), (1, 2), (1, 3), (2, 2), (3, 3)} belong to the Cartesian product $A \times B$, they are not in the relation. We would expect a predicate to define which ordered pairs are in the relation. Consequently, another way of looking at the concept of a relation is as a mapping to the Boolean set, {T, F}. This set consists of the truth values, **true** and **false** as shown in Fig. 4.3.

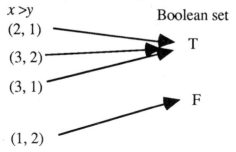

Fig. 4.3 'Greater than' mapped to the Boolean set

We can see that we could define a relation as a particular type of function which maps to the Boolean set. However, it would be unusual to use this approach in a **Z** specification, because it would be more straightforward to use a predicate to define the membership of a relation and the Boolean set would have to be introduced as a basic type as it is not part of the **Z** language.

4.3 The formal definition of relations

As with functions we need a formal definition of relations. Let A and B be sets. The relation R from A to B is a subset of $A \times B$ and we write $a \underline{R} b$ if $(a, b) \in R$. When the elements a and b are not related we write this as $(a, b) \notin R$. The statement $a \underline{R} b$, where $\underline{R}$ is an infix relational symbol, is a predicate that a is related to b in some specific way. The assertion is either **true** or **false**. In **Z** infix relation symbols are indicated by using an identifier underlined to show that it is being used as a relation, so that $(a, b) \in R$ means the same as $a \underline{R} b$.

In a relation elements can be related to other elements of the same set. Thus, for the 'greater than' relation, $m > n$ for any pair of integers drawn from the set $\mathbb{N}$, we could write $3 > 2$ or $3 \underline{R} 2$. In this case $\underline{R}$ represents the infix relation 'greater than'. When the relationship is between two sets or two elements of the same set we call it a **binary relationship** and $A \leftrightarrow B$ is the set of binary relations between A and B. Each such relation is a subset of the set $A \times B$ of ordered pairs. The type of a relation in **Z** is taken as $\mathbb{P}(A \times B)$, however it is more usual to give the type as $A \leftrightarrow B$ in a declaration by writing

$R : A \leftrightarrow B$

since this is more informative.

The same technical terms, such as domain and range, are used to describe features of both functions and relations. The domain of a relation is the set of all the members of the source which are related to at least one member of the target. The range is the set of all the members of the target set to which at least one member of the source is related. The **relational image** of a source produced by a relation is the set of all the objects which are related to one particular element of the source. In **Z** the relational image is indicated by the use of special brackets as shown below for the *Son_of* relation between the sets *M* and *S*:

$$Son\_of : M \leftrightarrow S$$
$$Son\_of \, (\!|\{Diana\}|\!) = \{William, Harry\}$$
$$Son\_of \, (\!|\{Anne\}|\!) = \{Peter\}$$

Notice by contrast that a function would give only a single value, the argument, as the relational image.

As we have seen in section 3.3 of chapter 3, the maplet notation $a \mapsto b$ is a graphical representation of the ordered pair (a, b). The formal definition of the image of the relation is given in **Z** notation as

$$R \, (\!|S|\!) \; == \; \{x : X, y : Y \mid x \in S \wedge x \mapsto y \in R \bullet y\}$$

where $R : X \times Y$ and $S : \mathbb{P}X$. This states that the relational image of a set *S* in *R* is defined so that when there is a *y* of type *Y* such that there is an *x* of type *X* in *S*, the ordered pair (x, y) exists in *R*. Now we can see that the relational image is a set, defined by set comprehension.

Example 1
The following are examples of different relations:

a) Set inclusion is a relation for any pair of sets. For sets *A* and *B*, either $A \subset B$ or $A \not\subset B$.

b) A set of pixels on a VDU screen. Consider two typical pixels *a* and *b* : either *a* is the same intensity as *b* or it is not.

c) Consider the two sets $A == \{1, 2, 3\}, B == \{a, b\}$ and a relationship $R == \{(1, a), (1, b), (3, a)\}$ which can also be written as a predicate: $1 \, R \, a \wedge 1 \, R \, b \wedge 3 \, R \, a$

A useful visual representation of a relation is through a diagram called a directed graph or a **digraph**. If we have a relation on a finite set *S* we can represent each element of *S* as a labelled dot called a node or a vertex; for example:

This digraph would represent the relation $\{(a, b), (b, c), (c, e), (d, a)\}$. The arrow linking the nodes is called the directed edge showing the relation is from a to b and not b to a. An element which is related to itself is shown by a self-loop, for example:

Although digraphs do not form part of a **Z** specification they are helpful for visualising different types of relations and for modelling specifications prior to using **Z**.

Functions can be conceived as special kinds of relations where an element of the domain maps to only one element of the range. Therefore many of the operations which were introduced when we considered functions can be applied to relations as well. This is essentially because for any two sets A and B for which we have f and g declared as:

$f : A \leftrightarrow B$
$g : A \rightarrow B$

both have the same type $\mathbb{P}(A \times B)$.

4.4 The composition of relations

It is often useful to combine relations in the same way that the compositions of functions operated in section 3.7 of chapter 3. We can form a new relation from the composition of two relations. In the audio music file there are sets *Artist, Title, Style*. A relation *Sings* maps *Artist* to *Title* as follows:

Sings == {*Betty Boo* $\mapsto$ *Boomania, Dreamland* $\mapsto$ *Blackbox,*
         Michael $\mapsto$ *Dangerous , Desree* $\mapsto$ *Mind Adventures,*
         Dire Straits $\mapsto$ *On Every Street, Michael Jackson* $\mapsto$ *Bad*}

There can also be a relation *Isa* between *Title* and *Style* as follows:

Isa == {*Boomania* $\mapsto$ *Rap/Dance, Dreamland* $\mapsto$ *Dance,*
       Dangerous $\mapsto$ *Pop, Mind Adventures* $\mapsto$ *Soul,*
       On Every Street $\mapsto$ *Rock, Bad* $\mapsto$ *Pop*}

The relational composition *Sings ⨟ Isa* will contain the following:

{*Betty Boo* ↦ *Boomania* ↦ *Rap/Dance,*
 Dreamland ↦ *Blackbox* ↦ *Dance,*
 Michael Jackson ↦ *Dangerous* ↦ *Pop,*
 Desree ↦ *Mind Adventures* ↦ *Soul,*
 Dire Straits ↦ *On Every Street* ↦ *Rock,*
 Michael Jackson ↦ *Bad* ↦ *Pop*}

The resulting relation will then consist of:

{*Betty Boo* ↦ *Rap/Dance, Dreamland* ↦ *Dance,*
 Michael Jackson ↦ *Pop, Desree* ↦ *Soul, Dire Straits* ↦ *Rock*}

Composition of relations has the same effect as functional composition. Naturally two relations can only be composed if the range of the first relation is the same as the domain of the second relation.

4.5 Inverse relations

Let R be a relation from A to B. The inverse of R, denoted by R^{-1}, is the relation from B to A consisting of those ordered pairs which, when reversed, belong to R. An alternative notation that is sometimes used for the inverse relation is $R^{\sim}$.

$$R^{-1} == \{b : B; a : A \mid (a, b) \in R \bullet b \mapsto a\}$$

For example, $>$ and $<$ are inverse relations.

If the relation R is of type $A \leftrightarrow B$ then the type of R^{-1} is $B \leftrightarrow A$ so that the inverse relation has ordered pairs with every element reversed:

$$y \mapsto x \in R^{-1} \Leftrightarrow x \mapsto y \in R$$

where, the reader will recall that the symbol $\Leftrightarrow$ was introduced in section 2.11 of chapter 2. This symbol can be read as 'if and only if' and states that the predicate on its left hand side is logically equivalent to the predicate on its right hand side.

Unlike the case of the inverse of a function, the inverse of a relation will always be another relation. Some relations will have inverses which are also functions. Recall that only injective functions have inverse functions.

Mother_of would be the inverse of *Son_of* and is given by:

$Mother\_of == Son\_of^{-1} == \{William \mapsto Diana, \ Harry \mapsto Diana,$
$\qquad\qquad\qquad\qquad\qquad Peter \mapsto Anne\}$

Exercise 1
(1) Find the inverse of the following relations:
(a) x is the husband of y
(b) x is taller than y

(2) Consider the relations, *Brother_of* and *Mother_of*, given by:
$\qquad Brother\_of == \{John \mapsto Lynne, Mike \mapsto Sue, David \mapsto Mary\}$
$\qquad Mother\_of == \{Lynne \mapsto Chris, Lynne \mapsto Matthew, Sue \mapsto Paul\}$

(a) using an appropriate name, write down the set definition of the
     inverse relation to *Brother_of*
(b) specify the blood relation defined by the relational composition
     Brother_of ⸵ Mother_of and write down its set definition

(3) For the vending machine described in example 6 section 3.6 of
     Chapter 3, write formal expressions for:

(a) a set *Charge* consisting of acceptable coins
(b) a relation, *Acceptable_coins*, defined in terms of its maplets to
     represent the different coins which can be combined to give the
     correct price

4.6 Projection of relations

An important requirement for the interrogation of relational databases is
the operation of projection when one or more columns (or tuples) are
selected from a data table. **Z** provides two special projection functions
which split ordered pairs into their first and second coordinates.

The projection function *first* will give the set of values corresponding to
the first member of an ordered pair.

$first : (X \times Y) \rightarrow X$

While the projection function *second* will give the second member of an
ordered pair.

$second : (X \times Y) \rightarrow Y$

As an illustration we can project the relations *Mother_of* (section 4.5)
and *Sings* (section 4.4) as follows:

$first(Mother\_of) = \{William, Harry, Peter\}$
$second(Mother\_of) = \{Diana, Anne\}$

and also,

$first(Sings) = \{Betty\ Boo, Dreamland, Desree, Dire\ Straits,$
$\qquad\qquad\qquad\qquad Michael\ Jackson\}$

$second(Sings) = \{Boomania, Blackbox, Dangerous,$
$\qquad\qquad\qquad\qquad Mind\ Adventures, On\ Every\ Street, Bad\}$

4.7 Domain restriction

In the music library example we established the sets *Artist* and *Song*. The relation which associates the artists with the number of songs on their CD is given by the following:

$tracks : Artist \leftrightarrow \mathbb{N}$

An example of *tracks* is:

$tracks == \{Blackbox \mapsto 7, Betty\ Boo \mapsto 11, Dire\ Straits \mapsto 12,$
$\qquad\qquad Desree \mapsto 10, Michael\ Jackson \mapsto 10,$
$\qquad\qquad Michael\ Jackson \mapsto 14\}$

If we are only interested in female artists then the relation can be restricted so the first elements of the ordered pairs belong to the set *Female*. This is **domain restriction** which is shown as $\lhd$. For example, if we let

Female : $\mathbb{P} Artist$ and $\{Betty\ Boo, Desree\} \subseteq Female$, then

$Female \lhd tracks = \{Betty\ Boo \mapsto 11, Desree \mapsto 10\}$

$Female \lhd tracks$ is a subset of the relation *tracks* which can be written as

$x \mapsto y \in Female \lhd tracks \Leftrightarrow \{x \in Female \wedge x \mapsto y \in tracks\}$

We may, however, be interested in the tracks of the non-female artists. This can be obtained by using an operation called **domain subtraction** shown as symbol $\ntriangleleft$. (This is also called **domain anti-restriction** or even domain **corestriction** in some texts). We could write:

$Female \ntriangleleft tracks = \{Dire\ Straits \mapsto 12, Michael\ Jackson \mapsto 10,$
$\qquad\qquad\qquad Michael\ Jackson \mapsto 14\}$

Since artists must be either male or female we can write

$$Male \cup Female = Artist$$
$$Male \cap Female = \emptyset$$

Female ◁ *tracks* is a relation which is a subset of *tracks* and

$$x \mapsto y \in Female \lhd tracks \Leftrightarrow \{x \not\in Female \land x \mapsto y \in tracks\}$$

4.8   Range restriction and anti-restriction

These are similar to the operations that can be performed on the domain. Using these operators we can subdivide the relation *tracks* so that, for example $x \mapsto y \in tracks$, if the artist x has made y tracks and it was decided that 10 was the average number of tracks on each CD.

$$Average == tracks \rhd \{10\}$$

Range **anti-restriction** is represented by the symbol $\rhd$.

$$Abnormal == tracks \rhd \{10\} = \{Betty\ Boo \mapsto 11,$$
$$Blackbox \mapsto 7,$$
$$Michael\ Jackson \mapsto 14,$$
$$Dire\ Straits \mapsto 12\}$$

Range anti-restriction is also known as range **corestriction** or range **subtraction**. To summarise, the symbols used in relational restrictions are as follows:

◁ domain restriction
◁ domain antirestriction
▷ range restriction
▷ range antirestriction

4.9 Relational overriding

The relation overriding operator ⊕ applies to relations in the same way as it does to functions, which is described in section 3.8 of chapter 3. However, in the case of relations, the relation $Q \oplus R$ relates everything in the domain of R to the same objects in R and in addition relates everything else in the domain of Q to the same objects as Q does. Q and R must be relations of the same type.

$$dom\ (Q \oplus R) = (dom\ Q) \cup (dom\ R)$$

This is different from the effect of functional overriding where the operator ⊕ will replace a maplet in the first function f with a maplet from the second function g. The extension of the concept of overriding to relations makes functional overriding a special case where the result must still be a function with the result that:

if $x \in \operatorname{dom} g$ then $(f \oplus g)\, x = g\, x$

4.10 Applications of relations

Relations can be identified in every database system. The **Z** functions described above provide the means to describe the major operations carried out on database systems i.e. updating and interrogating which are based on selection and projection. We will illustrate these concepts in the following examples.

Example 2
This is a simple supplier table consisting of the suppliers' code, which acts as a unique key to the table, and the suppliers' name.

Code of Supplier	Name
B63	Green
B35	Brown
A60	Smith
A40	Jones

In this example the set, *Supplier*, is given by:

$$Supplier == \{(B63, Green), (B35, Brown),$$
$$(A60, Smith), (A40, Jones)\}$$

We now consider a number of operations that can be performed on this database of information.

a) Let us suppose that a new supplier Norton, with code A20, is to be added to the file using relational overriding. This operation is given in **Z** by:

$$Supplier \oplus \{A20, Norton\}$$

with the result that

$$Supplier = \{(B63, Green), (B35, Brown), (A60, Smith), (A40, Jones),$$
$$(A20, Norton)\}$$

In this example a new supplier is added to the relation and this could have been expressed by set union as an alternative to relational overriding. However when we want to change existing data set union would give the wrong result because it would merely add another maplet. This is particularly dangerous in the case of functions which could be changed into relations by this operation. The next example illustrates this idea.

b) Now let us suppose that the supplier Smith changes its name to Bright. The supplier code is a function of the supplier's name and in this case functional overriding removes the ordered pair (*A60, Smith*) and replaces it with the ordered pair (*A60, Bright*).

Supplier ⊕(*A60, Bright*) = {(*B63, Green*), (*B35, Brown*),
(*A60, Bright*), (*A40, Jones*), (*A20, Norton*)}

c) A list of the suppliers' names is required for a report. This can be achieved with the projection function, *second.*

report = second(Suppliers) = {*Green, Brown, Bright, Jones, Norton*}

d) A user wishes to know the supplier code of Brown. This time we are going to use range restriction and then the projection function, *first.*

selection = Supplier ▷ {*Brown*} = {*B35, Brown*}

first(selection) = {*B35*}

4.11 Classes of binary relations

We can classify binary relations by examining their digraphs and this process will help to understand further the relationships being modelled. In contrast to functions which are often used to model dependencies between sets, relations are frequently used to compare elements of the same set or type. In the case where we want to model relations between sets of objects of the same type, it is possible to identify different classes of relations. A relation *R* in which every element is related to itself is called a **reflexive** relation and this is illustrated in the digraph below. When at least one of the nodes is not a self-loop the relation is **irreflexive**.

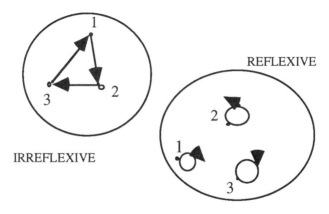

REFLEXIVE

IRREFLEXIVE

In **Z** there is a special relation called an identity relation **id** which maps every member of the domain to itself. For example the reflexive digraph above could be given as

id {1, 2, 3} = {1 ↦ 1, 2 ↦ 2, 3 ↦ 3}

We say that R is **symmetric** if whenever $(x, y) \in R$ then we also always have $y\,R\,x$. When no members can be related in this way the relation is **asymmetric**. The digraph of a symmetric relation is shown by a double arrow. A symmetric relation will arise when an object is described as having the same quality as another object or belonging to the same group, for example students in the same class.

SYMMETRIC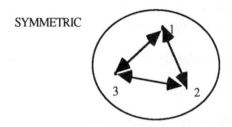

A third type of relation occurs when we have $x\,\underline{R}\,y$ and $y\,\underline{R}\,z$ and we can also say that $x\,\underline{R}\,z$. This is called a **transitive** relation. The numerical relational operators > and < are **transitive**. For example, taking $\underline{R}$ to be the infix relation 'less than', the digraph below shows that $1\,\underline{R}\,2$, $2\,\underline{R}\,3$, $1\,\underline{R}\,3$ and hence this is an example of a transitive relation.

TRANSITIVE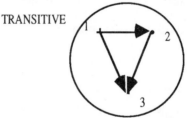

4.11.1 Closure

It is possible to convert a relation into a transitive relation by adding maplets. For example, if we consider the relation 'less than or equal to' defined by the set $R = \{1 \mapsto 2, 3 \mapsto 3\}$ we need to add two further maplets, $2 \mapsto 3$ and $1 \mapsto 3$, to make the relation transitive. In **Z** the notation R^+ is used to represent the operation of **transitive closure**. A transitive closure of a relation R is the smallest possible set created from R by the addition of further maplets ensuring that the new larger relation is transitive. In some texts this is called the strongest relation containing R which is transitive.

It would be possible to add further maplets to R to make the relation both reflexive and transitive. In the case of the digraph above we need to add the maplets $\{2 \mapsto 2, 1 \mapsto 1\}$. This operation is called **reflexive transitive closure** and is denoted in Z by R^* and it is the strongest relation containing R which is both transitive and reflexive.

Example
If A is the set of all the people in the country and x_1 and x_2 are any two members, the relation R maps x_2 to x_1 so that x_2 is the *mother of x_1*. When we classify this relation we see that it is not reflexive because in reality no one can be his/her own mother, and the relation is irreflexive. Also we know that if x_2 is *the mother of x_1*, then x_1 cannot be the *mother of x_2*, therefore the relation is not symmetric. Finally we recognise that if x_2 is the *mother of x_1* and x_1 is the *mother of x_3* we would not be able to say that x_2 is the *mother of x_3*. Therefore the relation is not transitive. To summarise *'mother of'* is irreflexive, not symmetrical and not transitive. In a specification there will be requirements which will dictate the classification of any relationship and it is good practice to analyse them in this level of detail.

Exercise 2
(1) A is the set of people in a country and x_1 and x_2 are any two
members of the set. Classify the following relations as reflexive, symmetric or transitive:

a) x_1 is taller than x_2

b) x_2 is the brother of x_1

c) x_1 is the wife of x_2

d) x_1 and x_2 go to the same college

e) x_1 is married to x_2

f) x_1 has the same blood group as x_2

4.11.2 Equivalence relations

A relation which is reflexive, symmetric and transitive is called an **equivalence** relation. We meet this type of relation often in everyday life and mathematics. We speak of two things being equivalent in the sense that one can be replaced by the other. An equivalence relation has a special definition so that when a relation is defined on a given set A by $x \underline{R} y$ then R is an equivalence relation when x is equivalent to y. Equivalence relations can only arise from sets of the same type.

Fig. 4.4 shows two examples of digraphs of equivalence relations from the relation $\{(1, 1), (2, 2), (3, 3), (1, 2), (2, 1), (2, 3), (3, 2), (1, 3), (3, 1), (4, 4)\}$.

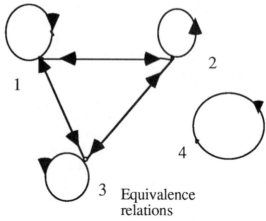

3 Equivalence
relations
Fig. 4.4

Fig. 4.4 shows that the relation could be partitioned into the equivalence
relations {(4, 4)} and {(1, 1), (2, 2), (3, 3), (1, 2), (2, 1), (2, 3),
(3, 2), (1, 3), (3, 1)}.

Some equivalence relations result in separating the original set into
subsets of the equal elements. For example if we have a relation on
people in the UK where x has the same number of children as y then
there will be several groups in the relation. One group will be made up
of people with no children, one with people who all have one child,
another for those with two children and so on. There are many similar
cases such as, for example, blood groups. To summarise: let R be a
binary relation on a set $A \times A$, then R is:

reflexive when for every $x \in A$, $x \underline{R} x$
symmetric when for every $x, y \in A$, $x \underline{R} y$ implies $y \underline{R} x$
transitive if for every x, y, z in A, $x \underline{R} y$ and $y \underline{R} z$ implies $x \underline{R} z$

A binary relation R on a set S is an equivalence relation if R is reflexive,
transitive and symmetric. An equivalence relation R on a set S
partitions the set into disjoint equivalence classes.

4.12 Changing relations into functions

In developing a systems specification, relations are more complex to
deal with than functions. It may be difficult to construct a predicate to
identify which members of the Cartesian product belong to the relation.
It is sometimes necessary to obtain a function from a relation in order to
implement a specification unambiguously. Often the inverse of a
relation will be a function and this is the simplest solution. In those
cases where the inverse of a relation is another relation there are a

number of methods which can be used in order to produce a function, such as:

A) For a relation which is not a function, define the equivalence relation which will partition the relation into equivalence classes. A representative set from each class will be a function with many of the same properties as the relation. For example, given the relation R as follows:

$R == \{(a, 1), (a, 2), (a, 3), (b, 2), (c, 3)\}$

This relation can be partitioned into classes e.g.

$\{(a, 1), (a, 2), (a, 3)\}, \{(b, 2)\}$ and $\{(c, 3)\}$

Then it is possible to select a representative of each class e.g.

$\{(a, 1), (b, 2), (c, 3)\}$

The result is a function.

B) Restrict the domain of the relation to remove the elements which map to more than one element of the range. Given the same relation R as above:

$R == \{(a, 1), (a, 2), (a, 3), (b, 2), (c, 3)\}$

In this method we would use domain restriction to exclude all maplets involving the element a to give a function, as shown below:

$\{a\} \vartriangleleft R = \{(b, 2), (c, 3)\}$

C) restructure the target set B to the power set of B which makes

$$f : A \to \mathbb{P}B$$
$$f : a \to \{b : \mathbb{P}B \mid a \underline{R} b\}$$

so that f is now a total function of $\mathbb{P}B$

We will now consider a detailed example of how these methods could be used in a specification where we need to model the relationship between suppliers and the products which they supply. In this system a supplier can supply many products, which in turn can be supplied by a number of suppliers, as shown in Fig. 4.6 below

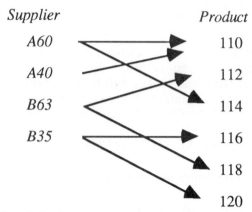

Fig. 4.5 Many to many relation

The relationship in Fig. 4.5 can be described as a relation, *Purchase*, such that

Purchase : *Supplier* ↔ *Product*

The relation, *Purchase*, will contain the following ordered pairs:

Purchase == {(*A60*, 110), (*A40*, 110), (*A60*, 114), (*B63*, 112), (*B63*, 118), (*B35*, 116), (*B35*, 120)}

In order to simplify the relation to produce a function we can use the methods described in A, B, C above, as follows:

Method A
Partitioning *Purchase* into disjoint sets will give:

{{(*A60*, 110), (*A60*, 14)}, {(*A40*, 110)}, {(*B63*, 12), (*B63*, 118)}, {(*B35*, 116), (*B35*, 120)}}

We will now select a representative tuple from each disjoint set . This gives the set:

{(*A60*, 110), (*A40*, 110), (*B63*, 112), (*B35*, 120)}

The result of this operation produces a function.

Method B

This is based upon restricting the domain to get rid of elements which map to more than one element of the range. In the case of *Purchase* it will be necessary to remove {*A60*, *B63*, *B35*}

{*A60*, *B63*, *B35*} ◁ *Purchase* = {(*A40*, 110)}

As we can see the use of either Method A or B with this relation will result in the loss of detailed information about the mapping between *Supplier* and *Product*.

Method C

The target set *Product* will be restructured to the power set of *Product*:

$f : Supplier \rightarrow \mathbb{P}\,Product$

This will give a total function. The result of this operation is shown in Fig. 4.6 below.

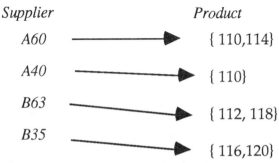

Fig. 4.6 Functional relationship

In this particular case Method C would produce the best solution as there is no loss of information as a result of the procedure. Every specification is different and the best method must be selected for each case.

4.13 Summary

The approach we have taken in this chapter has been to consider relations described as subsets of the Cartesian product of sets. It is possible to conceive of functions as special types of relations where the elements of the domain map to one and only one element of the range. If *F* denotes the set of all functions and *R* the set of all relations, using set notation we can write

$$F \subset R$$

and this can be shown using a Venn diagram in Fig. 4.7 below.

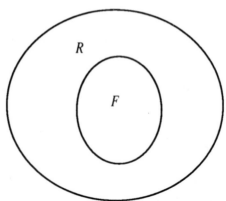

Fig. 4.7 Functions as a subset of relations

Relations and functions are sets of ordered tuples. Functions and relations are both subsets of the Cartesian products of sets. All functions are relations but only certain relations are functions. A relation can be conceived of as a function from a set of ordered tuples to the set {T, F} consisting of the truth values **true** and **false**. Functions are just special kinds of relations so that many relational operators such as ◁ and ⊕ can be used both on functions and relations.

Exercise 3

(1) Taking set $A == \{a, b, c, d, e\}$ and $B == \{1, 2, 3, ...20\}$, write a formal expression for a relation from A to B.

(2) Using the relations, *Brother_of* and *Mother_of*:

Brother_of == {*John* ↦ *Lynne, Mike* ↦ *Sue, David* ↦ *Mary*}
Mother_of == {*Lynne* ↦ *Chris, Lynne* ↦ *Matthew, Sue* ↦ *Paul*}

   (a) verify that
   $(Brother\_of \, \mathbf{\mathring{,}} \, Mother\_of\,)^{-1} = (Mother\_of^{-1} \, \mathbf{\mathring{,}} \, Brother\_of^{-1})$
   (b) state what sort of blood relationship is defined by
   $(Brother\_of \, \mathbf{\mathring{,}} \, Mother\_of\,)^{-1}$

(3) (a) Find the transitive closure of the relation defined by:
   PowersOfTwo == {2 ↦ 4, 4 ↦ 8, 8 ↦ 16, 16 ↦ 32}

   (b) Suppose the symmetric relation, R, is defined by:

   $R == \{2 ↦ 4, 4 ↦ 8, 8 ↦ 4, 4 ↦ 2\}$

   (i) find the transitive closure of this relation
   (ii) find the reflexive transitive closure of the relation

(4) Taking the set:

>   *Towns* == {*Hatfield, StAlbans, Luton, Bedford, Hitchin,*
>   *Dunstable*}

define a relation, $\underline{R}$, on *Towns* such that $x \underline{R} y$ if x and y are in the same County.

(a) show that $\underline{R}$ is an equivalence relation
(b) list the equivalence classes of *Towns*

(5) The teaching rooms in a university are booked to different courses. Only Science courses can book rooms which are laboratories. Write formal expressions for the following:
(a) the relation *book* between courses and rooms
(b) the relation *book* restricted to laboratories
(c) the relation *book* restricted to Science courses
(d) a further relation *make* which links time sessions to courses
(e) the composition of *make* with *book* to give the time slots when rooms are booked

(6) The Chinese lunar calendar dates from 2637 BC. Twelve animal signs are assigned to twelve different years forming part of a sixty year cycle. Chinese astrology is based on the year of a person's birth, believing that the animal ruling the year in which a person is born will have a profound influence over their life. For example, the latest cycle started in 1984 with the year of the *Rat*. The twelve signs can be represented by the set:

Sign == {*Rat, Ox, Tiger, Rabbit, Dragon, Snake, Horse, Sheep,*
      Monkey, Rooster, Dog, Boar}

Given a pre-defined set *Person* and a set *Year* of type $\mathbb{N}$, use $\mathbb{Z}$ notation to describe the following relationships and operations:

(a) *Birth* between *Person* and *Year*
(b) *Fate* between *Year* and *Sign*
(c) the sign of a person can be identified from his year of birth
(d) give a person's *Sign* when his year of birth is known
(e) write an expression for the addition of a new birth in the family
(f) obtain the number of members of your family who do not have the sign *Rat*

5

An Introduction to Z

5.1 Introduction

In this chapter we extend the use of the concepts developed in previous chapters, set theory, functions and relations, to show their usage in the formal specification language **Z**. This specification language is amongst the most widely used of specification languages today. Formal methods are increasingly being used in the development of safety critical software systems and **Z** is playing a leading rôle in this.

We discuss the following points, often using a music library scenario as a vehicle:

♦ the importance of typed sets in **Z**

♦ basic types which need to be declared - examples given from the music library

♦ the structure of a **Z** schema - having a declarations section and a predicate section

♦ the use of **Z** in writing specifications

♦ the incorporation of the principal decorations into **Z** schemas

♦ the Δ and Ξ conventions

5.2 The use of typed sets

In the **Z** language objects are specified as being members of **typed** sets, which were explained in chapter 2. When we define a variable in **Z**, we must always give its **type**. This is true no matter whether the variable takes elementary values or whether the variable takes sets as values. By declaring the type we specify the set which is known to contain the value of the variable.

There is a number of advantages in having the type system required by **Z**. The most obvious one to specification writers is that it allows a useful checking procedure which can detect certain kinds of errors in the specifications we write. Clearly, some errors are purely typographical, but, on the other hand, they might also reveal more serious problems caused by either a lack of fundamental understanding of the problem or a confused and muddled train of thought in thinking about the problem. Checking that a specification is correct in its type allocation is quite a straightforward matter and can now be performed by automated systems as well as human checkers.

A further advantage of the use of typed sets is that it enforces a certain structure on the specifications thus produced and imposes a discipline in the way they are written. This is especially useful when the specifications ultimately lead to computer programs which are written in a language which is itself typed.

There are also more theoretical reasons why typed sets should be employed. These reasons have to do with arguments involving Russell's paradox, and are beyond the scope of this book. The reader is encouraged to refer to a specialist text on logic for a description of this problem, and how the use of typed sets can overcome it.

5.3 Types

In general, we need to declare in advance all the types we might use when we write a **Z** specification. However, there are a couple of useful exceptions, namely **integer**, which has the symbol $\mathbb{Z}$, and **natural**, with the symbol $\mathbb{N}$. $\mathbb{Z}$ is an example of what is known as a **maximal** type, since it contains within it another type, $\mathbb{N}$, as a subset. These are known as **built in types** and were explained in chapter 2. **Natural** is used very frequently in **Z** specifications. The symbol $\mathbb{N}_1$ is also often used to denote the set of natural numbers which excludes zero.

Z allows the following normal arithmetic operations to be applied to objects of type **integer** and its subsets:

+	addition
-	subtraction
*	multiplication
÷	division (of integers)
mod	modulus (remainder after division)

These operators submit to the normal rules of precedence.

Z notation has no built-in type which denotes the set of **real** numbers. If a specification needs to use real numbers, the type *Real* can be defined as required.

Types which are not in-built need to be declared. They can be declared in two ways.

• Firstly, we can declare **basic types** or **given sets.** Here, we do not concern ourselves with what form the elements might take, we merely state the name of the type (conventionally beginning in capital letters) in square brackets. For example, the set of people (persons) that might become members of a music library would be declared as:

$$[Person\,] \qquad \text{the set of all possible unique persons}$$

Note the convention that a singular noun is used, and the comment that indicates the intended meaning.

• The second method of declaring types is by enumeration. This gives what is called a **free type**. For example, if the previously mentioned music library's recordings are available in one or more of a number of formats, we would declare the type:

$$Format ::= LP \mid CD \mid MC$$

where *LP, CD* and *MC* are the conventional recording industry descriptions of formats which are or have been widely available.

5.4 Variables

In **Z**, all names denoting values must be declared as belonging to a type. For example, we might introduce a named value (or variable) *mem* to represent a member of the music library and we say that *mem* is to be of the basic type *Person*, by writing:

$$mem : Person$$

In English, we would say that *mem* is a value contained in the set of possible values *Person*. More simply, we could say that a member (*mem*) is a *Person*. Another statement, apparently with a similar meaning, would be:

$$mem \in Person$$

Although the two statements *mem* : *Person* and *mem* ∈ *Person* seem to be broadly equivalent, there is an important difference in usage when we write **Z** specifications. The first (*mem* : *Person*) is used in the declaration part of a specification, when variables such as *mem* are being declared for the first time and we wish to know what type they belong to. The type, in this case, *Person*, must have been introduced previously **as a type**. The second statement (*mem* ∈ *Person*) is used when we are describing properties of variables which may or may not be true. As we shall see later, this is done in what is known as the predicate part of the specification. In this latter case *Person* would not be a previously declared type, but instead would be a previously declared variable.

A value could be given to *mem* by writing:

$$mem = \text{"John Smith"}$$

This assumes *John Smith* is a member of *Person*. We can go further and also define the variable *member*, the set of all members of the library, as having the type power set of *Person*:

$$member : \mathbb{P}\,Person$$

In other words the membership of the club is made up of a number of persons, each of whom belongs to the set *Person*. Again, a broadly equivalent statement, useful in predicates, would be:

$$member \in \mathbb{P}\,Person$$

$\mathbb{P}\,Person$ would, in this case, not be a type. It is just the power set of a set *Person*, which itself may have been declared as belonging to another type. Power sets were described in detail in chapter 2.

5.5 Schemas

When we write a specification in **Z**, we use a combination, on the one hand, of natural language and, on the other hand, of mathematical descriptions, which are written in the **Z** notation.

Z employs its own special way of distinguishing these two strands of the specification. The mathematical parts of such a specification use **schemas.** Interspersing these **schemas** are paragraphs of explanatory text in natural language.

An example of a schema follows:

```
┌─SomethingSimple ──────────
 mem : Person
├───────────────────────────
 mem ∈ member
└───────────────────────────
```

In this simple example we have introduced a schema called *SomethingSimple* and in the upper part of the schema we have declared a variable *mem* as being of type *Person*. In other words we have stated that a member is a person. Declarations such as this are always written in the upper part of the schema. A schema may have many such declarations.

The lower part of the schema is known as the **predicate** part. Here we write constraints that exist about the variables just declared, relating them to previously declared types or variables if necessary. In this case we have stated that *mem* must belong to the set previously declared, which we called *member*.

In drawing the lines of the schema, we usually extend them to reach the longest line of the declarations or the predicate part.

It is sometimes more convenient to write schemas in the *linear* form as:

$$SomethingSimple \; \hat{=} \; [\, mem : Person \mid mem \in member \,]$$

The operator $\hat{=}$ means "is defined as" and indicates textual equivalence. The linear form of schema must be written with square brackets around the right hand side of the equation as shown.

Generally a schema has the form:

```
┌─SchemaName ──────
│ declarations
├──────────────────
│  predicate
└──────────────────
```

The form of a linear schema is:

$$SchemaName \; \hat{=} \; [\, declarations \mid predicate \,]$$

It is possible to have schemas with no predicate part, which would simply declare new variables.

Readers familiar with programming languages such as Pascal will have noted the similarities between declaring a variable in **Z** with declaring one in a structured programming language. As in such languages the concept of scope is also inherent in **Z**. Variables declared within a schema are **local** to that schema. For a variable to be available to other schemas it needs to be imported. This will be covered later as we proceed through this chapter.

A simple way to make variables available, as any programming language student will know, is to make the variables **global**. We have effectively already done this to two variables earlier in this chapter when we defined *mem* and *member*. They became global variables by simply declaring them (writing them down) free from any enclosing schema. Note that values of *mem* are all single elements, whereas values of *member* are sets of elements. Both *mem* and *member* are still variables, not types, though they are of different type. *mem* is of type *Person*, whilst *member* is of type $\mathbb{P}\,Person$.

It is also possible to add constraining predicates to global variables as follows:

| *declarations*
| ―――――――――――
| *predicate*

Here the top and bottom enclosing lines present in a normal schema are absent to indicate the global scope of the variables. As an example of this we might want to specify that the number of borrowers from the library must not exceed the number of members of the club as:

| *borrowerList* : $\mathbb{P}\,Person$
| ――――――――――――――――――――
| $\#borrowerList \leq \#member$

When several variables are declared in a schema, each declaration usually occupies a single line, and the lines are regarded as being separated by a semi-colon. The semi-colon is not usually written unless schemas are written out in linear form. When the predicate part contains two or more lines, the lines are regarded as being joined by a logical **and** symbol or $\land$. This symbol will be covered more extensively in following chapters. Again the $\land$ is not normally written unless the schema is being shown in linear form. Thus:

```
┌─SomethingMore ―――――
│ borrower : Person
│ mem : Person
│ ―――――――――――――
│ borrower ∈ member
│ mem ∈ member
└──────────────────
```

can be read as equivalent to:

```
┌─SomethingMore ─────────────────┐
│ borrower : Person              ;
│ mem : Person
├────────────────────────────────
│ borrower ∈ member              ∧
│ mem ∈ member
└────────────────────────────────
```

The schema *SomethingMore* declares two variables *borrower* and *mem* in the upper part, and in the lower part states that both *borrower* and *mem* must be elements of the set *member* declared earlier.

5.6 The music library - brief specification

We now move on to write **Z** schemas to describe our music library in a more useful fashion than the fragmented extracts quoted in earlier sections. This music library has a number of **members** who may take out on **loan** various **copies** of **recordings** held by the library. Additionally **members** may make **reservations** for particular **recordings**.

We would like the specification initially to record facts like the above about the library. Other facts will be introduced later. The attentive reader might easily argue against some of the simplifications introduced at this stage in describing the library. However, we prefer to start from simple beginnings and then to enhance the specification later on. It is one of the strengths of **Z** that this process can be done in a relatively straightforward manner. Not all the facts need to be present or encapsulated when we start. Further elucidations can be incorporated at a later stage, as we shall show in subsequent chapters.

The reader will also notice that, when attempting to describe subsequent **Z** schemas in English, more information is provided than was given initially. This is because, when we write **Z** schemas, we are forced to think again about what is being written and to clarify exactly what we mean. This is yet one more argument in favour of **Z** and, indeed, of formal methods in general. They demand a precision of thought which otherwise could be lacking.

5.7 The music library - state invariant

The ensuing **Z** text sets out to state certain facts about the library and in common with all **Z** specifications, the mathematics is interspersed with natural language text.

We first declare the **basic types** which can be used in the remainder of the specification:

[*Person, Recording, Copy*]

As before, *Person* is the set of all possible unique persons. Likewise *Recording* is the set of all possible unique recordings. *Copy* is the set of identifiers that this library uses to distinguish all the different physical copies of the recordings. We do not need to know at this stage exactly what this set of identifiers consists of.

We now write a schema known as the **state invariant**. It is so called because it captures many of the important features of the state of our music library. In particular it ensures that statements are written down about features of the music library system which do not change no matter what actions might be performed later. It incorporates statements about the library which should always be **true**.

MusicLib	1.
member : $\mathbb{P}\,Person$	2.
held : $Copy \twoheadrightarrow Recording$	3.
loan : $Copy \twoheadrightarrow Person$	4.
reservation : $Recording \leftrightarrow Person$	5.
dom *loan* $\subseteq$ dom *held*	6.
ran *loan* $\subseteq$ *member*	7.
dom *reservation* $\subseteq$ ran *held*	8.
ran *reservation* $\subseteq$ *member*	9.

To help in the explanation of this schema, line numbers are printed in bold on the right hand side. These would not normally be included in a **Z** specification and are here purely to assist the beginner.

5.8 Explanation of music library state invariant

• Line 1 contains the title of the schema as a whole, *MusicLib*. This will be used in the succeeding text when we wish to refer to the whole schema.

In the upper part of this schema we have defined all the variables we are going to use in terms of previously declared types. These types must be either free types, basic types or built in types, as discussed in section 5.3 above.

• Line 2 repeats the declaration of the variable *member*. It is declared as being of type power set of *Person*. It is thus one of the many subsets of *Person*. In other words *member* is a set of elements, each of which represents a person.

• Line 3 denotes the function *held*. The library may hold a number of copies of each recording. This line records which recording is associated with each copy identifier. Further, the fact that it is a partial function (↦) means that not all copy identifiers are actually used by this library. The library does not have a copy of every recording made.

• Line 4 declares the *loan* function between the sets *Copy* and *Person*. A particular copy can only be out on loan to one member, and a person might borrow a number of copies of recordings. However, not all library copies are out on loan, which makes this a partial function. This library has not yet set a limit to the number of loans that a person can have outstanding.

We might want to write line 4 as *loan* : *Copy* ↦ *member*. This, however, is not good **Z** style, since we have to define all objects in terms of **types**. *member* has not been declared as a type, whereas *Person* has been so declared. The constraint that we only lend to members is covered by the predicate line 7, see below.

• Line 5 declares a relation, *reservation*, between *Recording* and *Person*. This reflects the fact that several different people might make reservations for the same recording and that one person might have reservations for different recordings.

A similar argument as above concerning line 4 prevents us from writing *reservation* : *Recording* ↔ *member* in line 5.

The lines that follow in the predicate part of the schema tie the previously declared variables together in a logical way.

• Line 6 constrains the domain of *loan* to be a sub-set of the domain of *held*. The domain of *held* is the set of copies of recordings actually held by the library, from line 3 above. This ensures the very reasonable requirement that the library only lends out items that it actually possesses.

• Line 7 ensures that the people involved in making loans are actually members of the library

• Line 8 constrains the domain of *reservation* to be a sub-set of the range of *held*. As in line 6 we would want to ensure that members only reserve recordings that the library actually holds.

• Line 9 again ensures that the people involved in making reservations are actually members of the library.

There is a further condition which we would like to impose on this music library. That is that we would want to ensure the very reasonable condition that reservations are only made for recordings of which all copies are out on loan. To do this, however, we need to involve the predicate calculus, which will be covered in chapter 6. Therefore we shall leave this extra constraint till later.

5.9 The delta (Δ) convention

In order to describe useful actions that the music library might undergo, we need to introduce the concept of **primed variables** and **primed schemas**. The **Z** convention is that when we write Δ*SchemaName,* we are creating an extra copy of the schema *SchemaName* written *SchemaName'*. Δ*SchemaName* will include both *SchemaName* and *SchemaName'*. Thus we can write:

```
┌─ΔSchemaName ───
│ SchemaName
│ SchemaName'
└──────────────
```

The Δ symbol is a **decoration** not an operator. The prime symbol (') is likewise another decoration. The Δ*SchemaName* schema is an example of **schema inclusion**, where one schema is defined in terms of one or more others. Schema inclusion is one of the great strengths of **Z** specifications. We can reuse previously written schemas in new ones. Further examples of this technique will be presented as we proceed.

The second copy of the schema, *SchemaName'*, is identical to the first except that all the variables are primed ('). This duplication extends to both parts of the schema. The declaration section of the primed schema declares all variables again but primed. The predicate section restates the same conditions but with all variables primed.

The convention is that whenever the system undergoes an operation or event, we can usefully write Δ*SchemaName* to help us describe the event. In Δ*SchemaName* the unprimed variables indicate the state of the system before the operation takes place, and the primed variables show the state afterwards.

To continue the music library example, the schema Δ*MusicLib* is written in expanded form below. In practice we would not write it out in full like this. Instead we would use schema inclusion. It is written in full here purely by way of explanation. Note also that in order to save space we have put two statements per line in the predicate. In doing so we have to separate them with the ∧ symbol, since both statements are **true**.

```
┌─ΔMusicLib ─────────────────────────────────────────────
│  member, member'              : ℙ Person
│  held, held'                  : Copy ⇸ Recording
│  loan, loan'                  : Copy ⇸ Person
│  reservation, reservation'    : Recording ↔ Person
├─────────────────────────────────────────────────────────
│  dom loan ⊆ dom held          ∧  dom loan' ⊆ dom held'
│  ran loan  ⊆ member           ∧  ran loan' ⊆ member'
│  dom reservation ⊆ ran held   ∧  dom reservation' ⊆ ran held'
│  ran reservation ⊆ member     ∧  ran reservation' ⊆ member'
└─────────────────────────────────────────────────────────
```

Now, whenever we write ΔMusicLib we can assume we have all the variables available as shown above and that all the predicate statements shown above also are **true**.

5.10 Initial state schema

When we write a full **Z** specification, we start, as mentioned in section 5.7 above by writing the types to be used and the state invariant schema. The next stage in writing a **Z** specification is to write what is termed the **initial state schema**. This is to give the whole system a starting point. In the case of our music library example it needs to show the situation that exists when there are, as yet, no members in the library, neither are there any recordings to be loaned. The schema is written below and is followed by the explanation.

```
┌─Init ─────────────
│  MusicLib'
├───────────────────
│  member' = ∅
│  held' = ∅
└───────────────────
```

Note that MusicLib', member' and held' are **decorated** with a prime (') symbol in this Init schema. This is because they represent the state of events **after** the initialisation has taken place. This concept was discussed in the previous section.

In the declarations section of the Init schema we have written MusicLib'. This means that Init is to include all the items incorporated within *MusicLib'*. In other words *Init* includes all five lines of the declarations of *MusicLib'* together with all five lines of the predicate part of *MusicLib'*. By doing this we have avoided having to write out all the lines of *MusicLib'* again. This is a further example of **schema inclusion.**

Init also includes the further constraints that both *member'* and *held'* are empty sets. Technically, we can regard the statements about the emptiness of *member'* and *held'* logically connected by an **and** (or ∧) both to each other and to the predicate constraints of *MusicLib*. **All** these statements are **true** in *Init*.

There is no need to write further constraints on *loan'* or *reservation'*, since the constraints of *Init* coupled with the those of *MusicLib'* ensure that both are empty.

5.11 An operation to change state

We can now write schemas which show operations or events that the music library might undergo. If we were writing the full specification for the music library, we would list all the actions that could take place and then write schemas for them all. Here we will illustrate the point by choosing just two examples: firstly, a new member joining the library, and, secondly, adding a copy of a recording to those held by the music library. Once again each schema is first written out and is then followed by an explanation. First the schema for a new member:

```
┌─AddNewMem ──────────────
│ ΔMusicLib
│ mem?  :Person
├─────────────────────────
│ mem?  ∉ member
│ member' = member ∪ {mem?}
│ held' = held
│ loan' = loan
│ reservation' = reservation
└─────────────────────────
```

In the first line of the above schema, we have written ΔMusicLib. As explained in the previous section, this means that *AddNewMem* will now include all the variables of *MusicLib*, both in unprimed (before) versions as well as primed (after) versions. Additionally all the predicates from *MusicLib* are included. This again is an example of schema inclusion, which is part of the schema calculus. Schema calculus is more fully explained in chapter 6.

The second line introduces the variable *mem?*, an input variable of type *Person*. The ? is not an operator of any kind. It forms an integral part of the variable name signifying that this is a variable being supplied as an **input** to the event. We assume that *mem?* is the new member who is about to join the library.

The first line of the predicate states a **precondition** that must obtain before the action can be considered valid. This particular precondition states that the new member must not already be a member of the library. In practice all schemas need preconditions. If preconditions have not been mentioned in earlier schemas, it is because the preconditions were always **true**. Note that in this particular schema we have not stated what would happen if the precondition stated should turn out to be **false**. This matter will be left to later chapters, as it can be considered when we introduce the schema calculus.

The second line of the predicate shows that the new version of the membership list, *member'*, is the same as the old one but augmented by union with the singleton set containing *mem?*. The remainder of the predicate shows that all the other variables are not changed by the action of a new member joining the library. We have to state quite explicitly what happens to all these other variables. If we do not do so, they remain undefined.

5.12 A further example of an operation to change state

We now write a schema to describe the situation which surrounds the addition of a copy of a recording to those already held by the music library:

$$
\begin{array}{l}
\hline
\text{AddCopy} \\
\Delta MusicLib \\
copyref?: Copy \\
record?: Recording \\
\hline
copyref? \notin \text{dom } held \\
held' = held \cup \{copyref? \mapsto record?\} \\
member' = member \\
loan' = loan \\
reservation' = reservation \\
\hline
\end{array}
$$

This schema also starts by calling Δ*MusicLib* with all that has been previously mentioned. The schema then goes on to introduce two variables *copyref?* and *record?* as inputs. The first of these is the reference identifier of the new copy which the library intends to use for the new item, and the second is the detail of the recording of which this is a copy .

The one line of precondition states that the *copyref?* proposed has not previously been used as a reference to a copy already in the library. There is no precondition to state whether or not the recording is already held in the library. The schema will cope with either possibility.

The remaining lines of predicate follow the pattern set by the predicate for *AddNewMem.* The *held* function is increased by the addition of the singleton set containing *copyref?* $\mapsto$ *record?* as a maplet. The remaining lines show that no changes take place to any of the other variables during the course of adding this new copy to the library. Recall that these lines cannot be left out of a Δ schema. Note that it does not matter whether or not any copies of the recording are already held by the library. This schema works for both cases.

5.13 The Xi (Ξ) convention

In this section we turn to consider how to write schemas where the variables do **not** change their values as a result of the event or operation under consideration. To do this we introduce the symbol, Ξ, another **decoration**. This is used when we wish to call up a schema which has already been defined, together with all its variables and predicate constraints, but to state that no change takes place to any of the variables while the operation takes place. The Ξ convention is used when we wish to make enquiries about the system, as we shall see in section 5.14.

When we write Ξ*SchemaName* we are creating a version of the schema *SchemaName,* which has two copies of every variable found in the original *SchemaName.* As in the Δ convention above, there are unprimed variables for the 'before' state and primed variables for the 'after' state. However, the Ξ convention goes further. When we use this, we also state that all the 'after' state variables (primed) have exactly the same values as in the 'before' state (unprimed). As with the Δ convention, section 5.9 above, the predicate statements are duplicated as well.

By way of example, the Ξ*MusicLib* schema follows, written out showing what it means in terms of our previous knowledge.

$$\boxed{\begin{array}{l} \Xi MusicLib \\ \Delta MusicLib \\ \hline loan' \quad = loan \\ member' = member \\ held' = held \\ reservation' = reservation \end{array}}$$

In a normal **Z** specification there would be no need to write all the above out in full. We would simply write $\Xi MusicLib$, and all the above schema is now implied without further complication. This convention can be used for any schema, where we wish to show that an operation can take place without change to any of the variables.

It can readily be seen that the Δ and Ξ conventions greatly reduce the amount of writing that has to be done when writing **Z** specifications, and help to encapsulate facts so that they can become readily available to writers of subsequent schemas.

5.14 Operations that do not change state

To illustrate the use of the Ξ convention, we will now write schemas which make enquiries on the music library.

In our first example we make an enquiry to determine who has borrowed a certain copy of a recording. In section 5.11 above we have already met the ? convention to denote variables supplied as input to an operation. In this example, we introduce the ! convention. The ! is used as **decoration** to denote variables which are returned as output from an operation. We write *copyref?* to denote the copy about which we are making the enquiry, an input to the operation, and *mem!* to denote the member who has the copy out on loan, the operation's output.

$$\boxed{\begin{array}{l} WhoHasCopy \\ \Xi MusicLib \\ copyref? : Copy \\ mem! \quad : Person \\ \hline copyref? \in \text{dom } loan \\ mem! = loan(copyref?) \end{array}}$$

This schema, *WhoHasCopy*, calls $\Xi MusicLib$ in the first line of the declarations section. In other words it makes available all the variables of *MusicLib*, both in primed and in unprimed versions, the associated predicates, and the fact that the primed variables have the same values as the unprimed versions. That is to say that nothing in the system changes as a result of making this enquiry.

The second line of declarations introduces the variable *copyref?* to denote the recording about which we are making the enquiry. The third line shows *mem!*, the member who has the particular copy out on loan. This is output as a result of making the enquiry.

The first line of the predicate section is a precondition which ensures that the requested copy is one which is in the domain of *loan*. The second line of the predicate shows the result of the enquiry. It is the image of the argument *copyref?* in the function *loan*. (Functions were described in detail in chapter 3.) The precondition is needed to ensure that the copy is actually out on loan. Otherwise, a *copyref?* which is not in the domain of the partial function *loan* will give an **undetermined** output, not simply a zero output.

The second example below, *ReservEnq*, is very similar in form to the previous schema, *WhoHasCopy*. *ReservEnq* returns a list of members that have the recording *record?* on reservation.

$$
\begin{array}{|l}
\hline
\text{ReservEnq} \\
\quad \Xi MusicLib \\
\quad record? : Recording \\
\quad list! \quad\; : \mathbb{P}\,Person \\
\hline
\quad record? \in \operatorname{ran} held \\
\quad list! = reservation (\!|\{record?\}|\!) \\
\hline
\end{array}
$$

The output, *list!*, is the output list of type $\mathbb{P}\,Person$. Again a precondition is needed to ensure that the recording is already in the library. The second line of the predicate returns the list required. This is the set obtained from the relational image of the singleton set {*record?*} over the relation *reservation*. It follows from the work on relations covered in chapter 4.

5.15 Summary

The chapter started by outlining how **Z** schemas are constructed and proceeded to show a number of typical schemas written to describe aspects of a music library system. Concepts introduced in earlier chapters were applied in developing these schemas.

The following new concepts were introduced during the course of the chapter: built in types, basic types, the structure of a **Z** schema including the linear form, the scope of variables, the prime (') symbol, the Δ and Ξ conventions and the ? and ! decorations.

These were used to write a state invariant schema, the initial state schema of the music library, schemas to describe operations that change the state of the system and schemas to describe operations that leave the system unchanged.

Exercise

(1) Write schemas similar to the *AddNewMem* and *AddCopy* schemas which capture the removal of a member and the removal of a copy from the system. Ensure appropriate preconditions.

(2) Write a further state invariant schema called *ArtistIndex* which incorporates a) the *MusicLib* schema and b) the idea of an index showing which artists perform on the recordings.

(3) Using the *ArtistIndex* schema above write a further schema to describe the operation of finding out what artists perform on a given recording - similar to *ReservEnq*.

(4) Using schemas already written, write a schema to describe the addition of a new recording to the library (*AddRec*).

6

Propositional and Predicate Calculus

6.1 Introduction

In the previous chapters we have dealt informally with simple predicates and the rules for combining them. The time has now come for these concepts to be put on a more formal and rigorous basis. It is necessary for us to do this because not only does **Z** use typed set theory, but, as we have seen in the previous chapter, the lower portion of a **Z** schema is reserved exclusively for the inclusion of predicates.

Propositional logic is concerned with the truth value of propositions and the rules of inference that enable us to make deductions. These ideas can be carried over into what is called **predicate calculus,** which allows us to reason and make deductions from a set of predicates.

In this chapter we consider the following:

♦ propositions and predicates

♦ truth tables

♦ disjunction and conjunction

♦ negation

♦ implication and logical equivalence

♦ quantifiers

6.2 Propositions and predicates

A proposition is a statement which can either be true or false. As an example, the following is a proposition:

Tomorrow is Monday

since it is an assertion which is either true or false. In contrast, the declaration, stop!, is not a proposition as it takes the form of a command. In practice it is much easier to have a label in order to refer to a proposition. For this purpose the convention is to represent propositions by single upper case letters.

We have already met the concept of a predicate in the earlier chapters in this book. It is time for us to clarify what exactly a predicate is and how it differs from a proposition. The distinction is that a predicate involves a formal variable which is presented to it in much the same way as an argument in a function e.g. $P(x)$ is a typical predicate asserting that x has the property P. Logicians, in fact, refer to $P(x)$ as an open sentence in the sense that it has no truth value attached to it as x refers to a 'dummy variable'. The truth value attached to $P(x)$ depends on the particular value that x is given when it is selected from a set of values. $P(x)$ can be evaluated as soon as the value of x is known. A proposition, on the other hand, is a statement without a variable. In practice we will be mainly concerned with predicates.

6.3 Conjunction and disjunction

Single predicates can be combined together in order to formulate more complex predicates. In English this is achieved by the use of key words such as *and* and *or* as **connectives** and these ideas with slight modification are carried over into propositional logic and predicate calculus.

Two predicates can be joined together by means of the operator, $\wedge$, to form a conjunction. The result of a conjunction of two predicates can be shown in a truth table where, for convenience, we omit the variable since we are only concerned with the truth value of the predicates.

P	Q	P $\wedge$ Q
T	T	T
T	F	F
F	T	F
F	F	F

Fig. 6.1　The conjunction of two predicates

In Fig. 6.1 each proposition is capable of independently assuming one of two truth values, T(**true**) or F(**false**). Consequently, there are exactly 2^2 (2×2) ways of combining these truth values where the power is determined by the number of propositions which in this case is

2, giving rise to a truth table consisting of 4 rows. The final column on the right gives the conjunction, P ∧ Q, of the truth values of P and Q from which we note that the conjunction is only **true** when both P and Q are **true**.

Each predicate occurring in the conjunction, P ∧ Q, is known as a **conjunct**. The order in which the conjuncts are written in a conjunction has no effect on its truth value. This can be seen from Fig. 6.1 as we can quite freely interchange the columns consisting of the truth values for P and Q without altering the overall truth value of the conjunction. An operation having this property is said to be **commutative**.

Example 1
The conjunction operation in predicate calculus is analogous to the logical AND operation in programming. For example, consider two functions in the programming language Pascal, $Even(x)$ and $Prime(x)$, which return either **true** of **false** depending on whether the value that replaces the formal parameter x when the function is called, satisfies the function.

In the same way that we can form the conjunction of two predicates in predicate calculus, we can construct a compound expression in programming by joining the two predicates together by means of the logical AND operator. Such an expression can be written as:

Even(GivenNumber) AND Prime(GivenNumber)

where GivenNumber is the name of an INTEGER variable in the program. The overall truth value of such a compound expression is decided by the truth table for conjunction and, as such, it will only be **true** when each individual conjunct is true and this will only occur when the value of the variable, GivenNumber, is 2.

Another connective operation is **disjunction**. The disjunction of two predicates P and Q is given by P ∨ Q where again, for convenience, we omit the variable. The individual predicates, P and Q, participating in the disjunction are known as **disjuncts**. We can show the result of a disjunction in a 2^2 truth table which covers all the possible combinations of truth values.

P	Q	P ∨ Q
T	T	T
T	F	T
F	T	T
F	F	F

Fig. 6.2   The disjunction of two predicates

From Fig. 6.2 we note that the only circumstance under which the disjunction, P ∨ Q, returns a **false** truth value is when both P and Q are **false**. We also observe from this truth table that if we interchange the columns containing the truth values of the disjuncts the truth value of the disjunction remains the same so that disjunction, like conjunction, is also commutative.

Example 2
The disjunction operation in predicate calculus is similar to the logical OR operation in programming. We can illustrate disjunction using the two functions, Even(x) and Prime(x), which we used in connection with conjunction. A disjunction involving these two functions can be written as:

Even(GivenNumber) OR Prime(GivenNumber)

where, once again, GivenNumber is the name of an INTEGER variable in the program. The truth value returned by this disjunction is **true** when GivenNumber is either even or a prime number and false otherwise.

6.4 Negation

The negation of a predicate, P, is indicated by placing the symbol ¬ before the predicate concerned and it serves the same function in predicate logic as *not* does in English. As such, negation acts as a **modifier** reversing the truth value of a predicate as shown in the truth table below:

P	$\neg P$
T	F
F	T

Fig. 6.3   The negation of a predicate

From this table we observe that the negation of a **true** predicate is **false**, while the negation of a **false** predicate is **true**.

Some simple examples of the negation of propositions are the following:

Proposition	The Negation of the Proposition
It is raining	It is **NOT** raining
The number of integers is finite	The number of integers is **NOT** finite

6.5 Implication

We have already met the connective operations of conjunction and disjunction which join together two propositions. Moreover, we have seen that the result of such operations can be displayed in a truth table. In this section we introduce another operator which, like conjunction and disjunction, is a connective placed between two propositions but which, in contrast to these earlier operators, is not commutative.

The operator we are going to consider is represented by the symbol $\Rightarrow$ and it is called by logicians 'implies'. It is a convenient name for summarising statements of the form '**if** P **then** Q'. We write, for example, $P \Rightarrow Q$ which means that the proposition P implies the proposition Q. There are many examples of such statements in everday use which fall into the 'if....**then**....' format and which can be captured by an implication statement. As an example we could consider:

'**if** it is raining **then** I will take my coat'

Using P to denote the proposition it is raining and Q to denote taking my coat, we can represent this symbolically as $P \Rightarrow Q$. In this context, P is called the **antecedent** and Q the **consequent** of the implication statement. If both P and Q are true, then $P \Rightarrow Q$ is also true as in the statement 'if a, b and c are the sides of a right angled triangle of which a is the hypotenuse, then $a^2 = b^2 + c^2$'. Conversely, if Q is false but P is true, we would naturally anticipate that the truth value of the implication statement is also false since we would not expect a false consequent to follow logically from a correct antecedent.

The above interpretation of the truth value of implies is in direct agreement with what we would anticipate. The interpretation, however, of the truth value of P $\Rightarrow$ Q is not so straightforward when P is false. As an example, we might consider the truth value of the statement 'if 3, 4 and 5 are the sides of an equilateral triangle, then $5^2 = 3^2 + 4^2$'. In this case the antecedent is false, the consequent true. The implication statement overall is taken to be true on the basis that we can make any deduction from a false antecedent irrespective of the truth value of the consequent.

P	Q	P $\Rightarrow$ Q
T	T	T
T	F	F
F	T	T
F	F	T

Fig. 6.4   The truth table for implication

6.6 Logical equivalence

Logical equivalence is yet another connector joining together two predicates. It is more straightforward than implication and easier to understand. We state that P is logically equivalent to Q if P $\Rightarrow$ Q and also Q $\Rightarrow$ P and we write P $\Leftrightarrow$ Q. From this definition of logical equivalence, we should anticipate that two predicates can only be logically equivalent if they have the same truth value.

The truth table for logical equivalence is shown below:

P	Q	P $\Leftrightarrow$ Q
T	T	T
F	T	F
F	F	T
T	F	F

Fig. 6.5   The truth table for logical equivalence

6.7 Tautologies and contradictions

A tautology is simply a statement whose truth value is always **true**. There are many examples of tautologies, involving a combination of several predicates. The best known example of such a tautology is the expression:

$P \vee \neg P$

The truth value of such a statement can be investigated by using a truth table as shown below:

P	$\neg P$	P $\vee \neg$ P
T	F	T
F	T	T

Fig. 6.6   A truth table for a tautology

It is seen from this table that the truth value of $P \vee \neg P$ is always **true**.

A concept closely related to tautologies is that of **contradictions**. A contradiction is simply a statement that is always **false**. The simplest such example of a contradiction is the expression:

$$P \wedge \neg P$$

The truth value of this statement can be investigated by using a truth table as shown below:

P	P	$P \wedge \neg P$
T	F	F
F	T	F

Fig. 6.7   A truth table for a contradiction

6.8 The universal quantifier ∀

We have already noted in section 6.2 the distinction between a proposition and a predicate. This difference can be summarised by stating that in the case of a predicate, there is a variable that can be associated with it. We now need to consider the values that can be given to such a variable and, in particular, the set from which those values can be drawn.

As an example, consider the statement that all even numbers have a remainder of 0 when divided by 2. In arithmetic there is an operation, mod, which returns the value of any remainder after division of one number by another. In particular, the remainder after dividing a number, x, by 2 is given by $x \bmod 2$. Hence, the condition for a number x to be even can be translated into the statement $x \bmod 2 = 0$.

Let us now introduce a predicate, $E(x)$, which returns **true** when x is an even number and **false** otherwise. The set of even numbers is an infinite subset of the set of integers $\mathbb{Z}$ and we can write

$$E(2) \wedge E(4) \wedge E(6) \dots \wedge E(100) \dots$$

If $x \in \mathbb{Z}$ we can select the even numbers by using the additional requirement that $x \bmod 2 = 0$ as a filter. These considerations lead us to the following statement which is true for all values of x satisfying the filtering predicate:

$$\forall x : \mathbb{Z} \mid x \bmod 2 = 0 \bullet E(x) \tag{6.8.1}$$

in which the special symbol, $\forall$, is literally equivalent to 'for all' and acts as a generalised conjunction. This statement breaks down into three components:

(a) the declaration of a universally quantified variable x viz: $\forall x : \mathbb{Z}$

(b) a filtering predicate, x mod 2, to select out those values of the universally quantified variable that give a remainder of 0 when divided by 2.

(c) the quantified predicate, $E(x)$, which occurs after the separator, $\bullet$, which must always be present.

The whole statement (6.8.1) can be read as 'for all x of type $\mathbb{Z}$ such that x mod 2 = 0, x has the property of being an even number'. Again, as in earlier chapters, we note the emphasis on typed sets that is one of the hallmarks of **Z**. The type declaration here ensures that the variable x is bound to values of the set $\mathbb{Z}$ throughout the entire statement and, for this reason, x is referred to as a **bound variable**. In contrast, variables not declared in any type statements before the constraint bar but which occur after the constraint bar are said to be **free variables** although they are, of course, still subject to the usual type constraints of **Z**. We will illustrate this difference shortly.

The illustration (6.8.1) exemplifies the general form of any statement involving the universal quantifier:

$$\forall D \mid P \bullet Q \qquad\qquad (6.8.2)$$

where D represents declarations, P denotes optional filtering predicates and Q is the quantified predicate.

In cases where there is no restriction or constraint on the quantified variable, the constraint bar can be omitted as no filtering predicates are required in these circumstances. A universally quantified statement, in this case, takes the simplified form:

$$\forall D \bullet Q \qquad\qquad (6.8.3)$$

with the same significance attached to both D and Q as previously given. A specific example of this form is given by:

$$\forall x : \mathbb{N}_1 \bullet x > 0$$

which is equivalent to the infinite conjunction:

$$(1 > 0) \wedge (2 > 0) \wedge (3 > 0) \wedge (4 > 0) \ ... \ (10 > 0) \ ...$$

As a more general example of a statement involving both a bound and a free variable, we consider the following:

$$\forall x : N_1 \bullet x > y$$

in which x is a bound variable because it is the subject of the universal quantification. In contrast, y is a free variable as it is not included within the scope of the universal quantification but it is still subject to the type constraints of **Z**. Moreover, we note that this particular example has no constraint as it involves all values of the set N_1 without exception. The predicate, however, may be either **true** or **false** depending on the value attached to the free variable y. If $y < 1$, the predicate will always return **true** since N_1 consists of the set of positive, natural numbers greater than zero. If $y > 1$, the predicate is **false**.

As a final illustration of the use of the form (6.8.3), we now reconsider the *square-op* schema presented in chapter 3:

```
┌─ square_op ──────────
│
│ n : N
│ absquare : N → N
│ ─────────────────────
│ absquare n = n²
└──────────────────────
```

This schema defines a function *absquare* which takes an element belonging to the set of natural numbers and returns its square. Using the universal quantifier, this can be written as:

```
┌─ square_op ──────────
│
│ absquare : N → N
│ ─────────────────────
│ ∀n : N • absquare n = n²
└──────────────────────
```

Note that the use of the universal quantifier in the predicate part of the schema removes the necessity for a type declaration in the signature block of the schema.

An equivalent expression to the general form (6.8.2) is given by

$$\forall D \bullet P \Rightarrow Q$$

so that the statement (6.8.1) about even numbers can also be written as

$\forall x : \mathbb{Z} \bullet x \bmod 2 = 0 \Rightarrow E(x)$

6.9 The existential quantifier ∃

In many situations we are unable to make statements that are universally true. However, we may know that the statement is true for particular values of the set under consideration. It is clear that in these circumstances, we require a different symbol from the universal quantifier and what we require is a quantifier that asserts that there is at least one value of the variable for which the quantified predicate is true. The predicate calculus provides an existential quantifier, ∃, which asserts that there exists at least one value of the existentially quantified variable that satisfies the predicate which follows after it.

The general form of any statement involving the existential quantifier is

$$\exists D \mid P \bullet Q$$

where, once again, as in the case of the universal quantifier, D represents declarations, P denotes optional filtering predicates and Q is the quantified predicate. An alternative form which removes the necessity of using the constraint bar is given by:

$$\exists D \bullet P \wedge Q$$

A simplification in the use of the existential quantifier occurs when there is no filtering predicate required, in which case, any statement involving the existential quantifier can be reduced to the form:

$$\exists D \bullet Q$$

An example of this simplified form of declaration with the existential quantifier is provided by:

$$\exists x : \mathbb{Z} \bullet x^2 = 100 \qquad (6.9.1)$$

which is satisfied when either $x = 10$ or $x = -10$.

In 6.8 we have seen that universal quantification over a set of values is equivalent to a conjunction taken over all values of the set. In a similar manner, existential quantification can be viewed as a shorthand notation for writing down a disjunction. For example, (6.9.1) is equivalent to the disjunction

... $(-10^2 = 100) \vee$ ...$(-5^2 = 100) \vee (-4^2 = 100)$ ... $(2^2 = 100)$ ...

which will return **true** provided one or more of the disjuncts has a **true** truth value.

Example 3

As an illustration of the use of the existential quantifier, consider a computer network with users able to gain access via a number of terminals. In order to restrict access, each user is given an account identifier which is based on their first name and surname. Moreover, in order to make each account secure, protection is provided by a password known only to the user of that account. This password consists of two alphanumeric characters followed by two numeric digits.

In order to gain entry to the network, each user must:

(a) enter the account name correctly
(b) enter the appropriate password for that account

Only after completion of steps (a) and (b) can the user gain access to the system. Furthermore, access is restricted at any given time to 50 valid users.

We can model this system by introducing a set, *Names*, consisting of the names of the valid users of the network. Typical entries in this set could be:

Names == {*DAllum, LDunckley, DHeath, ...*}

and it is known that #*Names* is far in excess of the maximum permissible number of users.

In addition to this set we need to introduce a set, *Passwords*, consisting of all the valid passwords required in order to gain access to the network. Each user of the system has a single password that enables access to the network. The same password may, however, be used by different users of the system. We can visualise this set as follows:

Passwords == {*ZW13, AW15, HM52, ...*}

Finally, we introduce a surjective function, *ValidUser*, which has the type $\mathbb{P}$(*Names* × *Passwords*), and is defined as:

ValidUser : *Names* →→ *Passwords*

The number of valid users currently using the system we can model by a set, *Users*, which will be a subset of the set *Names*. This set will be continually updated as users leave and enter the system. Consequently, we have:

$$\exists x : Names \mid (y : Passwords \quad \bullet \quad y = ValidUser(x)) \wedge x \notin Users$$
$$\wedge \ \#Users < 50 \bullet Users' = Users \ \cup \ \{x\}$$

in which the filtering predicate is a conjunction ensuring that the password matches up with a user not currently using the system and the number of users is less than 50. If both of these conditions are satisfied then the user is able to gain access to the network. The reader will note that in this example, the variable y is not quantified and has to be declared on the right hand side of the constraint bar.

6.10 The unique existential quantifier $\exists_1$

The existential quantifier, $\exists$, asserts that there is at least one value of the variable in the declaration part satisfying the quantified predicate. At least one value signifies there are one or more values which can satisfy the quantified predicate. In some cases, we may wish to be more precise and specify that there is just one unique value which satisfies the quantified predicate. In such cases we can use the unique existential quantifier, $\exists_1$, which states that there is one and only one value, which can be be drawn from the declaration part to satisfy the quantified predicate. Again, as in the case of existential quantification, there are two forms that any statement involving the unique existential quantifier can take depending on whether optional filtering predicates are required or not.

As an example of the use of the unique existential quantifier, we can consider the following:

$$\exists_1 y : \mathbb{N} \mid x \in \mathbb{N} \bullet x / y = x$$

which states that there is at exactly one value, y, drawn from the set of natural numbers such that any value, x, selected from the natural numbers has its value unchanged when it is divided by y. The filtering predicate is in this case $x \in \mathbb{N}$ and the quantified predicate is $x / y = x$ which is of course satisfied when $y = 1$.

6.11 Negation of the universal quantifier

There is a simple rule to deal with the negation of a universally quantified predicate which we will now deduce. Consider the statement 'all PCs have a floppy 5.25" disc drive' which can be formally stated in predicate calculus as:

$$\forall x : PersonalComputers \bullet DiscDrive(x)$$

where the set, *PersonalComputers*, consists of all the personal computers ever manufactured and *DiscDrive(x)* is a predicate which evaluates to **true** when x is selected from the set *PersonalComputers* and has a 5.25" floppy disc drive and evaluates to **false** otherwise. In most cases the truth value returned will be **false** as most PCs now only have a 3.5" disc drive.

The negation of 'all PCs have a floppy 5.25" disc drive' is 'not all PCs have a floppy 5.25" disc drive' which is equivalent to 'there exist PCs without a 5.25" disc drive'. The predicate calculus translation of this statement is:

$$\exists x : PersonalComputers \bullet \neg DiscDrive\ (x)$$

From this particular result we observe that moving the negation operator 'inwards' to the other side of the universal quantifier results in replacing the universal quantifier by the existential quantifier and negating the quantified predicate. In the case where an optional filtering predicate is included, this remains unchanged as it is only the quantifier and its associated quantified predicate which are affected.

As an example of the negation of a universally quantified predicate with a filtering predicate, we will return to the earlier example (6.8.1):

$$\forall x : \mathbb{Z} \mid x \bmod 2 = 0 \bullet E(x)$$

which states that all integer numbers, x, satisfying the filtering predicate are even numbers, $E(x)$. This statement is true for all values of x which pass through the 'filter'. The negation of this statement is:

$$\neg(\forall x : \mathbb{Z} \mid x \bmod 2 = 0 \bullet E(x)) \tag{6.11.1}$$

which we expect to return false for all filtered values of x. The negation of the quantified predicate, $E(x)$, is $\neg E(x)$ and, as we have seen, when the negation is moved to the other side of the universal quantification, the universal quantifier is replaced by the existential quantifier. The filtering predicate remains unchanged with the result that we have:

$$\exists x : \mathbb{Z} \mid x \bmod 2 = 0 \bullet \neg E(x)$$

as the negation of the original statement (6.8.1).

In summary, we have the following results:

Statement	Negated statement
∀ D • Q	∃ D • ¬ Q
∀ D| P • Q	∃ D| P • ¬ Q

. **Fig. 6.8**   The negation of a universally quantified predicate

6.12 Negation of the existential quantifier

In the last section we looked at the negation of a statement involving universal quantification, and we must now look at the analogous rule for the negation of statements involving the existential quantifier. In order to guide us in the deduction of a general rule for the negation of existentially quantified predicates, we consider the statement 'there exists at least one PC without a floppy 5.25" disc drive'. This can be formally stated in predicate calculus as:

$$\exists \, x : PersonalComputers \; \bullet \; \neg DiscDrive(x)$$

where the set *PersonalComputers* and the predicate *DiscDrive(x)* have the same meaning as in the previous section.

The negation of 'there exists at least one PC without a floppy 5.25" disc drive is 'all PCs have a floppy 5.25" disc drive'. Hence, we have the result:

$$\neg(\exists x : PersonalComputers \bullet \neg DiscDrive(x)) \Leftrightarrow$$
$$\forall x : PersonalComputers \; \bullet \; DiscDrive(x)$$

Again, as in the previous section, we observe that moving the negation operator 'inwards' results in replacing the existential quantifier by the universal quantifier and negating the quantified predicate. In this example, we have $\neg(\neg DiscDrive(x))$ i.e. double negation of the quantified predicate, giving simply *DiscDrive(x)*.

We can summarise the results of this section in a similar way to that of the previous section:

Statement	Negated statement
$\exists\, D \bullet Q$	$\forall\, D \bullet \neg Q$
$\exists\, D \mid P \bullet Q$	$\forall\, D \mid P \bullet \neg Q$

Fig. 6.9   The negation of an existentially quantified predicate

6.13 Universal and existential quantification

The predicates that we have looked at in previous sections have all involved quantification by either the universal or the existential quantifier. In this section we consider predicates that are quantified by a mixture of quantifiers. As an example, we might consider the following statement:

$$\forall\, x : \mathbb{N}, \exists\, y : \mathbb{N} \; \bullet \; x/y \in \mathbb{N}$$

which involves both the universal and existential quantifiers. This predicate asserts that all members of the set of natural numbers, $\mathbb{N}$, are exactly divisible by at least one number of the set $\mathbb{N}$. In the case of prime numbers this is true when either $x = y$ or $y = 1$. In the case of composite numbers, which can be factored into the product of prime numbers, this is true when y is any prime factor of x. The order in which the quantification is carried out is implied by the order of the quantifiers. Firstly, a particular x value is selected from $\mathbb{N}$ and then, secondly, the predicate asserts that there is at least one value of the set $\mathbb{N}$ which will divide exactly into x. This is repeated for all x in $\mathbb{N}$.

We will now consider the effect of interchanging the order of quantification with the result that we have:

$$\exists\, y : \mathbb{N}, \forall\, x : \mathbb{N} \bullet x/y \in \mathbb{N}$$

This statement is only satisfied when $y = 1$. The implied order in the quantification is, in this case, to select a y value which will in all cases divide all the natural numbers exactly.

In this example we observe that interchanging the universal and existential quantifiers results in the predicate being true for a different set of values with the result that we cannot in general state that

$$\forall\, x : \mathbf{N},\, \exists y : \mathbf{N} \bullet x/y \in \mathbf{N} \Leftrightarrow \exists y : \mathbf{N},\, \forall\, x : \mathbf{N} \bullet x/y \in \mathbf{N}$$

This example shows that due caution must be exercised when interchanging the order of quantification and the reader is recommended to treat each individual case on its own merits.

6.14 Summary

This chapter has introduced a number of operators and logical connectives that can be used to combine propositions. We have seen that a predicate, $P(x)$, is really a proposition asserting that the variable x has the property P with a truth value determined by the particular value that x is given. In practice, the variables presented to a predicate are usually quantified over a set of values given in a type declaration. We shall see in the following chapters that quantified predicates are very important and useful in the construction of $\mathbf{Z}$ schemas.

Exercise

(1) Using truth tables verify that $\neg(P \wedge Q) \Leftrightarrow \neg P \vee \neg Q$

(2) Using a predicate Rainy(x), where x is drawn from the set:

> *DaysInWeek* == {*Sunday, Monday, Tuesday, Wednesday, Thursday, Friday, Saturday*},

write down the following statements:

   (a) it will rain on *Monday*
   (b) it will rain every day of this week
   (c) it will rain at least once during this week
   (d) it will rain on exactly one day of the week

(3) Let P(x) denote the predicate asserting that x is a prime number and E(x) the predicate that x is an even number. Using these predicates, state the truth value of the following statements and if they are either tautologies or contradictions:

   (a) $\forall x : \mathbb{N} \bullet P(x) \wedge E(x)$
   (b) $\exists_1 x : \mathbb{N} \bullet P(x) \wedge E(x)$
   (c) $\forall x : \mathbb{N} \bullet P(x) \vee E(x)$
   (d) $\forall x : \mathbb{N} \bullet P(x) \wedge \neg E(x)$
   (e) $\exists x : \mathbb{N} \bullet P(x) \wedge \neg E(x)$
   (f) $\forall x : \mathbb{N} \bullet P(x) \vee \neg P(x)$
   (g) $\forall x : \mathbb{N} \bullet E(x) \wedge \neg E(x)$

(4) As we have seen in Chapters 3 and 6, schemas can be used to define functions. Using the universal quantifier, write the schema block for *cube_op* using a function $cube(x) = x^3$ with a domain and range consisting of the natural counting numbers.

7

Z Schema Calculus

7.1 Introduction

In previous chapters we introduced the **Z** language (chapter 5) and the ideas of propositional and predicate calculus (chapter 6). We now go on to use these concepts to expand our notions of the **schema calculus**. The schema calculus is the system of rules that we use to combine previously defined schemas together to produce new ones. Some of these rules have already been touched on in chapter 5.

The advantages of using a schema calculus are easy to understand. When we combine schemas together we are reusing concepts which have already been expressed in some schema or other. We do so without going to the lengths of writing out all the previous schemas again. We can thus express new ideas in a compact yet logically consistent form.

The chapter starts with the revision of a number of points from chapter 5, which are nevertheless part of **Z** calculus. These include:

♦ schema decoration - using the example of the schema *MusicLib'*

♦ schema inclusion - including the examples of the Δ and Ξ conventions

The chapter then goes on to introduce further topics from the **Z** schema calculus, illustrating them with new examples from the music library scenario:

♦ schema conjunction and disjunction - using examples concerning non-standard or error conditions

♦ other logical connectives - the implication, equivalence and negation operators

♦ schema renaming - creating a schema entitled *YoungMusicLib* based on the original *MusicLib*

♦ schema hiding and projection operators - making selected variables local to an existential quantifier within a schema predicate

♦ schema composition - combining two schemas, *AddCopy* and *AddNewMem*, into a new schema, *Gift*.

♦ systematic renaming - where all variables within a schema with a certain decoration or subscript are renamed to exactly the same names, but with a different decoration or subscript

♦ schema piping - the similarity between this and composition is emphasised

♦ schema preconditions - describing the relationships which must exist between the various components of a schema, including the components of **included** schemas, and its inputs for the operation described by the schema to apply

7.2 Schema decoration

We now review the ideas of the schema calculus that have already been covered in chapter 5. The first of these is **decoration**. This is a simple idea, and when it is used it is generally associated with some action or other taking place in the real world. Chapter 5 (section 5.9) shows an example of this when describing the Δ convention. Here the schema *MusicLib'* (the **decorated** schema) is identical with schema *MusicLib* except that all the variables contained within the former are decorated with a prime (') or dash. The primed schema and the primed variables signify the values of the schema and the variables after some operation has been carried out. The unprimed (undashed) values are associated with the state before that particular operation.

7.3 Schema inclusion

The second idea from chapter 5 is that of **schema inclusion.** Here the name of a previously declared schema is included in the declarations of a new schema. This has the effect that the previous schema is textually imported *in toto*; its declarations are merged with those of the new schema, and its predicate part is conjoined (see subsequent section 7.5) with that of the including schema.

Chapter 5 has many examples of schema inclusion. For example, section 5.9 defines Δ*MusicLib* by including both *MusicLib* and *MusicLib'*, section 5.10 defines *Init* by including *MusicLib'*, while defining further predicates, and section 5.11 includes Δ*MusicLib* in its definition of *AddNewMem*.

Both the Δ convention and the Ξ convention of chapter 5 depend on the inclusion of **decorated** schemas.

7.4 Schema conjunction

A new concept is that of **schema conjunction**. This is the use of the conjunction symbol ($\wedge$) from chapter 6, and is used when we wish to define a new schema from two previously defined ones. For example, we might have a new schema W, say, to be defined as the conjunction of two further schemas S and T:

$$W \cong S \wedge T$$

The new schema W is made up as follows. Firstly, the declaration parts of the two schemas S and T are merged to make up the declaration part of schema W. Secondly, the predicates of S and T are conjoined to make up the predicate of W. Thus, if we have:

```
┌─S ─────────────
│ Sdeclarations
│
│ Spredicate
└─────────────
```

and:

```
┌─T ─────────────
│ Tdeclarations
│
│ Tpredicate
└─────────────
```

We can make up W as follows:

```
┌─W ─────────────
│ Sdeclarations    ;
│ Tdeclarations
│
│ Spredicate      ∧
│ Tpredicate
└─────────────
```

Conjunction can only legally be done when variables which have the same name in the declarations of both the two starting schemas (S and T) are of the same type. Otherwise the operation is illegal.

7.5 Schema disjunction

Schema disjunction is very similar to schema conjunction as above
in section 7.4. In the case of schema disjunction we might have as our
example:

$$W \cong S \vee T$$

Here the declarations of S and T would be merged to form the
declaration of W, and, in this case, the predicates of S and T would be
disjoined to form the predicate of W. The resulting W in this case
would look like:

```
┌─W─────────────────
│  Sdeclarations    ;
│  Tdeclarations
├───────────────────
│  Spredicate      ∨
│  Tpredicate
└───────────────────
```

Again it is only legal if variables with the same name in the two
schemas S and T are of the same type.

7.6 Examples using conjunction and disjunction

To illustrate the use of schema conjunction and disjunction we
consider again a schema from chapter 5. Section 5.11 shows the
schema *AddNewMem*. For convenience it is repeated again below.

```
┌─AddNewMem─────────────────
│  ΔMusicLib
│  mem?  :Person
├───────────────────────────
│  mem? ∉ member
│  member' = member ∪ {mem?}
│  held' = held
│  loan' = loan
│  reservation' = reservation
└───────────────────────────
```

We notice that the first line of the predicate serves as a precondition
that the person wishing to join the library is not already a member.
This line is:

$$mem? \notin member$$

In order to provide a fuller specification we need to consider what to do if the precondition is not met. In other words we need to write down what would happen should the person *mem?* turn out to be already a member; that is:

$$mem? \in member$$

In these circumstances it would be reasonable to output a message of some kind. We therefore define a new enumerated type as follows:

$$Response ::= OK \mid alreadyMember$$

We can now write an error handling schema to handle the case where the person wishing to join is already a member:

```
┌─AddNewMemError ─────────────
│ ΞMusicLib
│ mem? : Person
│ reply! : Response
├─────────────────────────────
│ mem? ∈ member
│ reply! = alreadyMember
└─────────────────────────────
```

The first line of the declaration of this schema, *AddNewMemError,* is the line:

$$\Xi MusicLib$$

This shows (see chapter 5, section 5.13) that no change takes place to any of the variables of *MusicLib* during the operation. In particular no change takes place to the list of members (*member*).

The second declaration line introduces the proposed new member (*mem?*).

The third declaration line declares the variable *reply!*. This will deliver an output of type *Response* after the operation.

The first predicate line now has the complementary precondition that the person **is** already a member. The second predicate line ensures an output reply '*alreadyMember*'.

We are now in a position to write a schema that encompasses the whole operation of adding a new member, whether or not the person (*mem?*) who wishes to join is already a member or not. We will call this operation *EnrolNewMem*.This name is chosen to distinguish it from the previous *AddNewMem*.

To complete the scenario we need to add a small schema to specify an output message for the non-error case as well, where the person joining is not already a member. For the sake of brevity, we write this in the linear form:

$$OKMessage \cong [reply! : Response \mid reply! = OK]$$

Now we write, using the schema calculus:

$$EnrolNewMem \cong (AddNewMem \wedge OKMessage) \vee$$
$$AddNewMemError$$

This is the normal way it would be written in a working **Z** specification. For completeness, however, the full schema *EnrolNewMem* is written out next:

```
┌─EnrolNewMem ─────────────────
│ ΔMusicLib
│ mem?  : Person
│ reply! : Response
├──────────────────────────────
│ ((mem?        ∉ member
│  member'      = member ∪ {mem?}
│  reply!       = OK)
│         ∨
│  (mem?        ∈ member
│  member'      = member
│  reply!       = alreadyMember))
│         ∧
│  held'        = held
│  loan'        = loan
│  reservation' = reservation
└──────────────────────────────
```

As the reader will appreciate, though, this is done purely for the purposes of exposition. Written out like this, the schema defeats the object of brevity which was stated as a reason in favour of the schema calculus in section 7.1!

7.7 Other logical connectives

In exactly the same way that we have used the conjunction and disjunction connectives ($\vee$ and $\wedge$) to join schemas together in Sections 7.4 and 7.5 above, we can use the other logical connectives of implication ($\Rightarrow$) and equivalence ($\Leftrightarrow$) to join schemas together. Additionally, the negation operator ($\neg$) can be used in front of schemas, as in the expression, $W \mathrel{\hat{=}} \neg S$.

We should be aware that, logically, both the implication connective ($\Rightarrow$) and the equivalence connective ($\Leftrightarrow$) can be built up from the conjunction connective ($\wedge$), the disjunction connective ($\vee$) and the negation operator ($\neg$).

The reader should be wary of using the negation operator at first reading since it can give rise to previously unsuspected complications. These complications apply also to the use of the implication and equivalence operators, but they can all be resolved by using the technique of **schema normalisation**, which will be covered in more detail in chapter 10.

7.8 Schema renaming

An existing schema can be used to create a new one of the same form but using different variable names by the simple technique of **schema renaming**.

In general, if we want to use an existing schema in the definition of a new one, the only difference between the two being one or more of the variables having a different name, we use the following convention:

$$NewSchema \mathrel{\hat{=}} OldSchema\,[newVarName\,/oldVarName\,]$$

Here the exact form of *OldSchema* is used to make the new schema (*NewSchema*), and every occurrence of the old variable name (*oldVarName*) in the existing schema (*OldSchema*) is replaced by the new variable name (*newVarName*) in the new schema.

As an example of this, we extend the idea of the music library to encompass another library which caters for young people. To make our task more comprehensible in this example, we assume that the young people have access to the very same stock of music recordings that other members are entitled to borrow. We can thus retain the variable *held* from the schema *MusicLib* introduced in chapter 5. However, we need to introduce the variable name *youngMember* to denote the membership list of young members. Additionally we need to have separate variables *youngLoan* and *youngReservation* to cater for the separate sets of loans and reservations that young people will make. We introduce the state invariant schema for this young person's music library as:

$YoungMusicLib \triangleq$
     $MusicLib\ [youngMember\ /\ member\ ,\ youngLoan\ /\ loan\ ,$
        $youngReservation\ /\ reservation\ ]$

This has the effect of creating a complete new schema identical to
MusicLib except that all the variables on the right hand side of the '/ '
symbols are replaced by the variables on the left hand side of the '/ '
symbols. For completeness of exposition the full *YoungMusicLib* is
written below. As explained earlier, however, this would not normally
be done as it defeats the object of brevity as stated in section 7.1.

$$
\begin{array}{|l l}
\hline
\multicolumn{2}{l}{YoungMusicLib} \\
youngMember & : \mathbb{P}\,Person \\
held & : Copy \nrightarrow Recording \\
youngLoan & : Copy \nrightarrow Person \\
youngReservation & : Recording \leftrightarrow Person \\
\hline
\multicolumn{2}{l}{\text{dom } youngLoan \quad \subseteq \text{dom } held} \\
\multicolumn{2}{l}{\text{ran } youngLoan \quad \subseteq youngMember} \\
\multicolumn{2}{l}{\text{dom } youngReservation \subseteq \text{ran } held} \\
\multicolumn{2}{l}{\text{ran } youngReservation \subseteq youngMember} \\
\hline
\end{array}
$$

7.9 Schema hiding operators

We often wish to 'hide' specified variables so that they are no longer
variables of the schema. Instead they become variables local to
existential operators (see chapter 6) in the predicate of the schema.
As an easy example we could write:

$$SomethingHidden \triangleq Simple \setminus (amem)$$

where *Simple* is the schema:

$$
\begin{array}{|l}
\hline
Simple \\
amem : Person \\
member\ :\ \mathbb{P}\,Person \\
\hline
amem \in member \\
\hline
\end{array}
$$

SomethingHidden thus becomes the schema, which **hides** the variable
amem :

```
┌─SomethingHidden ──────────────────
│ member : ℙ Person
├──────────────────────────────────
│ ∃amem : Person • amem ∈ member
└──────────────────────────────────
```

With more complex schemas several variable names could be written in the hiding brackets and thus only be seen locally inside existential statements.

Should we wish, we can hide all **but** named variables using the technique of **projection**. As another easy example we may write:

$$SomethingElseProjected \cong Simple \restriction (member)$$

With the same *Simple* as we have just used, this would give the resulting schema, which **projects** the variable *member* :

```
┌─SomethingElseProjected ──────────
│ member        : ℙ Person
├──────────────────────────────────
│ ∃amem : Person • amem ∈ member
└──────────────────────────────────
```

Further examples of hiding will be outlined in the next two sections.

7.10 Schema composition

When we use the concept of schema composition, we are defining a schema W, say, which encapsulates the actions of one schema, say, S, followed immediately by another, say, T. We would write:

$$W \cong S \mathbin{\fatsemi} T$$

The very fat semi-colon '⨟' is the symbol for schema composition. Implicit in the use of composition is the idea that we are not interested in the intermediate effects of what happens after S and before T. In order for composition to work, we have to ensure that the dashed (after) names of the first schema must match exactly the undashed (before) names of the second.

Effectively, the composition operator performs the following:

a) It renames all the **after** (dashed) variables of S to some temporary values

b) It renames the **before** (undashed) variables of T to the **same** temporary values. It should be noted that if the two sets of variables are not exactly the same the composition is undefined and in fact would make no sense

c) The new schema W then **includes** both the revised S and the revised T.

d) The temporary names are hidden with an existential quantifier in this new schema

e) Simplification is then performed on this new schema W, eliminating as far as possible all the temporary variables

To illustrate this we consider the schemas that describe the actions whereby a previously unregistered member may make a gift of a copy of a recording to the music library and thus, in recognition of his/her generosity, automatically gain membership of the library. We could therefore define:

$$Gift \cong AddCopy \,\mathbin{\S}\, AddNewMem$$

We have already defined both $AddCopy$ and $AddNewMem$ in chapter 5. Please note that, for the sake of clarity, this example does not consider non-standard or error conditions. We now go through the steps of composition of $AddCopy$ and $AddNewMem$ with the steps as described above:

a) We write down the revised version of the first schema of the composition, $AddCopy$. In order to maintain readability we shall use the double prime symbol " to indicate these temporary variables and call the revised schema $AddCopy["/\,']$. This is a convenient way of indicating that all the primed variables of $AddCopy$ have been transformed to double primed variables in $AddCopy["/\,']$, and is an example of what is known as **systematic renaming**. Thus we have:

```
┌─AddCopy["/ ']─────────────────────────
│ MusicLib ; MusicLib"
│ copyref?        : Copy
│ record?         : Recording
├───────────────────────────────────────
│ copyref?        ∉ dom held
│ held"           = held ∪ {copyref? ↦ record?}
│ member"         = member
│ loan"           = loan
│ reservation"    = reservation
└───────────────────────────────────────
```

b) Now we write down the revised version of the second schema *AddNewMem*. This is referred to as *AddNewMem*["/]. Again this is a convenient way of indicating that all the unprimed variables in the original version are converted to double primed variables in the new one, and is a further example of **systematic renaming**. For the original version of *AddNewMem*, please refer to chapter 5, section 5.11.

```
┌─AddNewMem["/ ]──────────────────
│ MusicLib" ; MusicLib'
│ mem?  :Person
├──────────────────────────────────
│ mem?          ∉ member"
│ member'       = member" ∪ {mem?}
│ held'         = held"
│ loan'         = loan"
│ reservation'  = reservation"
└──────────────────────────────────
```

c) The next stage is to write the new schema, *Gift*, which **includes** *AddCopy*["/ '] and *AddNewMem*["/].

```
┌─Gift────────────────────────────────────
│ ΔMusicLib
│ copyref?      : Copy
│ record?       : Recording
│ mem?          : Person
├──────────────────────────────────────────
│ ∃MusicLib"  •
│        mem?          ∉ member"
│        copyref?      ∉ dom held
│        held"         = held ∪ {copyref? ↦ record?}
│        member"       = member
│        loan"         = loan
│        reservation"  = reservation
│        member'       = member" ∪ {mem?}
│        held'         = held"
│        loan'         = loan"
│        reservation'  = reservation"
└──────────────────────────────────────────
```

Note that in this schema, the double primed variables are hidden in the predicate by using the existential quantifier statement:

∃*MusicLib"* • ...

In this way *MusicLib"* has been removed from the declaration section. Recall that:

$$\Delta MusicLib \;\hat{=}\; MusicLib \; ; \; MusicLib'$$

d) We now attempt to eliminate the double primed variables within the schema generated by step c) by considering the equalities within its predicate:

```
┌─Gift ──────────────────────────────────────────
│  ΔMusicLib
│  copyref?        : Copy
│  record?         : Recording
│  mem?            : Person
├──────────────────────────────────────────────────
│  ∃MusicLib"  •
│          mem?            ∉ member
│          copyref?        ∉ dom held
│          held'           = held ∪ {copyref? ↦ record?}
│          member"         = member
│          loan"           = loan
│          reservation"    = reservation
│          member'         = member ∪ {mem?}
│          held'           = held
│          loan'           = loan
│          reservation'    = reservation
└──────────────────────────────────────────────────
```

The ∃*MusicLib"* quantification can now be eliminated, since each double dashed variable is equal to one of the plain or dashed variables. The quantification carries no further useful information:

```
┌─Gift ──────────────────────────────────────────
│  ΔMusicLib
│  copyref?        : Copy
│  record?         : Recording
│  mem?            : Person
├──────────────────────────────────────────────────
│  mem?            ∉ member
│  copyref?        ∉ dom held
│  held'           = held ∪ {copyref? ↦ record?}
│  member'         = member ∪ {mem?}
│  held'           = held
│  loan'           = loan
│  reservation'    = reservation
└──────────────────────────────────────────────────
```

This final schema *Gift* is the composition of *AddCopy* and *AddNewMem*. It can be seen that the schema could easily be written out directly without the rigmarole of going through all the steps a) to e). This is usually the case with most practical schemas where there is a need to go through composition. However, it is still theoretically necessary to understand the steps, since cases might occur where they would be needed.

7.11 Schema piping

A very similar concept to schema composition is that of schema **piping**. Here the first schema's output variables, those decorated with a !, are matched with the second schema's input variables, those decorated with a ?. Those that match are then renamed to the same new names, and hidden in a new schema created by the conjunction of the two original schemas. Finally the new names are removed as much as possible by simplification, in a similar manner to that which happens in composition.

The symbol for **piping** is '»' as in:

$$W \cong S \gg T$$

The difference between composition and piping is as follows. Composition acts upon those variables which are (or may be) changed by the two operations in question (primed and unprimed variables). Piping, by contrast, is used when the variables in question are inputs and outputs to the two operations (variables decorated with ! or ?), and is not as common in practice as composition. Both operations involve the use of **hiding** as described in section 7.9.

7.12 Schema preconditions

This operation is used when we wish to compute the precise conditions under which a certain operation is applicable. The operator is known as the schema precondition (written **pre**), and can only be applied to schemas that represent operations. It is constructed by hiding all the variables of the schema which correspond to 'after' states and all those which are outputs (decorated with a !). As in composition and piping, we also try to simplify the expressions as much as possible.

As an example, we take the previously written schema *WhoHasCopy* for the music library (from chapter 5) and attempt to find a precondition for it. *WhoHasCopy* is repeated next:

```
┌─WhoHasCopy ──────────────────
│ ΞMusicLib
│ copyref? : Copy
│ mem! : Person
├──────────────────────────────
│ copyref? ∈ dom loan
│ mem! = loan(copyref?)
└──────────────────────────────
```

Thus   *preWhoHasCopy*   would be:

$$WhoHasCopy \setminus (mem!)$$

which is:

```
┌─preWhoHasCopy ───────────────
│ MusicLib
│ copyref?        : Copy
├──────────────────────────────
│ ∃MusicLib' ; mem!     : Person •
│     copyref?      ∈ dom loan
│     mem!          = loan(copyref?)
└──────────────────────────────
```

We can now go further than this and 'unpack' the quantified *MusicLib* schema:

```
┌─preWhoHasCopy ──────────────────────────────────────
│ MusicLib
│ copyref?        : Copy
├──────────────────────────────────────────────────────
│ copyref?        ∈ dom loan
│ ∃member'        : ℙ Person ; held' : Copy ↠ Recording ;
│     loan' : Copy ↠ Person ; reservation' : Recording ↔ Person ;
│       mem! : Person | MusicLib'Predicate  •
│             mem!           = loan(copyref?)
│             loan'          = loan
│             member'        = member
│             held'          = held
│             reservation'   = reservation
└──────────────────────────────────────────────────────
```

Here we have written *MusicLib'Predicate* to stand for the invariant which *MusicLib'* is required to satisfy.

Recall that *preWhoHasCopy* does not describe a change of state. What it does is to describe the relationship which must exist between the various components of the *MusicLib* state and the input *copyref?* for the operation *WhoHasCopy* to apply.

While writing the above schema we separated out those conjuncts which made no mention of dashed components. We can eliminate the existentially quantified variables if we satisfy two conditions: firstly that we can express these variables in terms of the *MusicLib* components and the input *copyref?*, and secondly that these values satisfy *MusicLib'Predicate*.

Clearly, the schema *preWhoHasCopy*, as written above, satisfies these two conditions. (See exercise 4.) We can therefore write the simplified schema:

```
┌─preWhoHasCopy───────────
│ MusicLib
│ copyref? : Copy
├──────────────────────────
│ copyref? ∈ dom loan
└──────────────────────────
```

It will not always be possible to entirely eliminate the dashed or output components in favour of the undashed or input ones. However, in practice it frequently happens this way. The reader will note the similarity of this exercise to those of composition and piping. In the former it is the double dashed components which are eliminated, and in the latter an arbitrary set of new names.

7.13 Summary

In this chapter we have brought together previously discussed ideas and have gone on to show additional ways of combining schemas. We used further examples from our music library to illustrate these.

The chapter started with the revision of a number of points including schema decoration, and schema inclusion. We then went on to introduce further topics from the **Z** schema calculus: schema conjunction and disjunction, the implication, equivalence and negation operators, schema renaming, the schema hiding and projection operators, schema composition, systematic renaming, schema piping and schema preconditions.

Exercise

(1) In a similar manner to section 7.6 above, which involves schema conjunction and disjunction, go through the arguments and produce schemas, based on *AddCopy* (as in chapter 5) and on others which you

might have to write support error messages, which take into account the possibility that a copy being added to the library is attempting to use a reference number which already exists.

(2) We might have the case where a member disappears while still having recordings out on loan. Using composition, write a new schema *MemberVanish* as a composition of two operations, one of which removes any recordings on loan to the member from the stock of the library and the other which removes the member from the list of members. Make sure, when you are writing these two preliminary schemas, that you give definitions that explicitly relate the before and after states. When writing the composed schema *MemberVanish*, ensure that you go through the full process of derivation as outlined in section 7.10 above.

(3) Satisfy yourself that the *preWhoHasCopy* schema **does** satisfy the conditions laid down in section 7.12.

(4) Write a precondition schema for *AddNewMem* (from chapter 5 section 5.11) using the same reasoning as in section 7.12 above.

8

Finite Functions and Sequences

8.1 Introduction

In the earlier chapters we discussed the concepts of sets, relations, functions and the way these can be defined and analysed using predicate calculus. We saw how these ideas could be applied to entities in applications such as the music library to model real life objects. For example in our file of compact disks in chapter 3 we noted how the relationships between the different attributes could be specified by the use of functions and relations.

When we use a set or a power set to model separate records in a data file we are restricted to just a few operations which can be carried out on sets. We can check for set membership and we can check the total number of elements within a set. However in most database systems this would not be good enough, we require concepts of greater expressive power. There is a need to model users' requirements, such as to retrieve a particular record in a data file, and for the modelling of this type of requirement to be as straightforward as possible. Bags and sequences are used in **Z** to overcome the limitations of basic set theory. As we shall see, bags and sequences are themselves specially defined functions and relations.

At the end of this chapter the reader should:

♦ understand the basic concepts of finite functions and sequences

♦ be able to define and classify different types of sequences

♦ understand the application of the different concepts of sequences to simple models

♦ be able to formalise the use of sequences in simple specifications

The purpose of this chapter is to consider more advanced concepts of functions and to introduce sequences. Bags are covered in detail in chapter 9. The chapter begins by extending the knowledge of the general concepts of functions gained in chapter 3 to special applications. We start by considering the case of finite functions because in many real applications we will only be interested in finite sets and the mappings between them. The later part of this chapter is concerned with the introduction of the concepts used to deal with sequences of objects in specifications.

8.2 Finite Functions

In applications it is sometimes important to restrict sets and functions to finite domains. A finite subset S of a set X is finite if the members of S can be counted, without repetition, by some natural number and this number is $\#S$, the cardinality of the set S. In $\mathbf{Z}$ finite sets are denoted by the use of the letter $\mathbb{F}$ in place of $\mathbb{P}$ as in the expression $\mathbb{F}X$, to mean the set of all the subsets of X. The non-empty members of $\mathbb{F}X$ are members of the set denoted by $\mathbb{F}_1 X$. We can formally define a finite set of X as follows:

$$\mathbb{F}X == \{S : \mathbb{P}X \mid \exists\, n : \mathbf{N} \bullet \exists\, f : 1..\,n \to S \bullet \operatorname{ran} f = S\}$$

This declares that $\mathbb{F}X$ is the set of all S where S is of type $\mathbb{P}X$, constrained by a function f which has as the domain, natural numbers from 1 to n where n is any natural number, and the range of the function is the set S.

In preparing specifications describing relationships between two sets X to Y we will usually only be interested in functions where the domain is a finite subset S of X which can be counted by some natural number. This number is the cardinality, $\#S$, of S. In $\mathbf{Z}$ the finite partial functions from X to Y are denoted in the way introduced in chapter 3, by the use of the special partial function arrows with the addition of a further vertical bar so that we can declare a partial finite function, using the symbol $\nrightarrow$:

$$X \nrightarrow Y == (X \rightarrow Y) \cap \mathbb{F}(X \times Y)$$

In the same way the set of finite partial injections is denoted as a subset of the finite partial functions which are also injections. We can then write

$$X \rightarrowtail\!\!\!\rightarrow Y == (X \nrightarrow Y) \cap (X \rightarrowtail Y)$$

8. 3 Inductively defined functions

As we found in chapter 3 a function from A to B can be defined by a predicate which will assign to each element of set A exactly one element in set B. However it is also possible to define a function inductively. This means we would define a finite function by defining the first few elements in the domain and range explicitly and then show that it is possible to apply a rule repetitively to compute the next member of the range in terms of the previously defined members.

This is technically referred to as proof by induction, since it provides a method of proving a given property holds for all members of a set.

Inductive definitions are valid for functions involving natural numbers and for finite sets. In the case of natural numbers every natural number from zero onwards can be defined by repeatedly adding a new number. Finite sets can also be inductively defined because every new member can be reached by repeatedly adding new members.

To define a finite function inductively, the procedure to follow to prove that a particular property P(x) holds over the domain, would be to show:

1) that P(0) holds

2) that P(x) holds for any member x of type $x : X$ and so does P(x +1);

We will illustrate this process in the next three examples which define selected functions for natural numbers.

Example 1
The first example is a simple function which we could define by set comprehension, as shown in chapter 3. This example will show how to use induction to define the simple function:

$$f == \{0 \mapsto 0, 1 \mapsto 2, 2 \mapsto 4, 3 \mapsto 6, ...\}$$

The domain and range are taken from the natural numbers and the function could have been defined in λ notation as:

$$f = \lambda n : \mathbb{N} \bullet 2n$$

The first step of definition by induction states the first member of the range as follows :

$$a) \quad f(0) = 0$$

The second step defines how the successive members of the range can be generated by adding 2 to the previous member.

$$b) \quad f(n+1) = f(n) + 2 \text{ for } n >= 0$$

This process would give a range of $\{0, 2, 4, 6, ...\}$

The next example uses induction for the definition of the factorial function $n!$ which would be difficult to define by set comprehension. Each member of the range is generated by multiplying the previous successive members of the range together with the argument so that while 2! is 2 the next member 3! becomes 6. This is another example in the case of the application of the concepts of proof by induction where the first member of the range is defined and it is shown that subsequent new members conform to the defined rule.

Example 2
The first step defines the first member of the range as follows:

a) factorial $(0) = 0! = 1$

the next member can now be shown to conform to the following rule:

b) factorial $(n+1) = (n+1)! = (n+1) \times$ factorial (n) for $n >= 0$

This shows the members of the range are $\{1, 2, 6, 24, ...\}$

In the final example it is necessary to declare the first two members and then apply the induction rule.

Example 3
The Fibonacci sequence is used in modelling many growing systems because the sequence describes population growth based upon the two previous members of the range.
Define $f: \mathbb{N} \to \mathbb{N}$

a) Let $f(0) = 1$ and $f(1) = 1$

b) if $x > 1$, let $f(x) = f(x-1) + f(x-2)$

Thus $f(2) = 1+1 = 2$, $f(3) = 3$, $f(4) = 5$ etc.

The range is $\{1, 1, 2, 3, 5, 8, 13, ...\}$

We will now apply the concepts of finite functions introduced in the last two sections when dealing with sequences.

8.4 Sequences

Sequences are special kinds of functions. Even when the user is interested in the whole set, the elements may be required to be presented in a specific order or sequence. In many real applications there are multiple objects with the same name, for example, in a library many books may be stored as multiple copies with the same title and authors. Each copy in the library should be arranged in the correct order on the shelves. Therefore the basic set operations available need to be extended to enable sequences of multiple copies to be modelled. It is, however, fundamental to the concepts of a set that each member is unique and that the members can be arranged in any order.

We can model a finite sequence based on any set by using a function from the set of natural numbers greater than zero to the set of interest. The function would be a partial function from a subset of the natural numbers to any set A in such a way that the members of set A can be linked to more than one natural number. In other words the function need not be an injection and this type of sequence is illustrated by the example below.

Example 4

This example is from the development of a model needed to describe the work schedules of a company. The set A is made up of the days of the week i.e. *Monday, Tuesday, Wednesday, Thursday, Friday, Saturday* and *Sunday*. The week-end days count as additional working days but no employee is allowed to work both week-end days in the same work period.

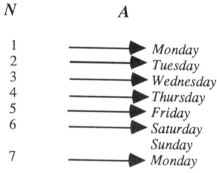

Fig. 8.1 Sequence Mapping

As the Fig. 8.1 shows a sequence can contain a repetition of a member of the range. In this example *Monday* appears twice while *Sunday* is omitted completely from the sequence.

We can see that a sequence of any set A is a function from $\mathbb{N}$ to the members of set A.

$$s : \mathbb{N} \to A$$

Sequences are special finite functions denoted by **seq** in $\mathbb{Z}$, so that seq A is the set of finite sequences over set A. The type of the sequence of any set A, seq A is $\mathbb{P}(\mathbb{PN} \times A)$ and the type of any sequence of values of type A is $\mathbb{P}(\mathbb{N} \times A)$. However, it is usual to declare a sequence s of elements of type A as s : seq A.

We can define a sequence t as a function using the maplet notation, as follows:

$$t = \{1 \mapsto 1,\ 2 \mapsto 4,\ 3 \mapsto 9,\ 4 \mapsto 16,\ 5 \mapsto 25\}$$

or as a subset of the Cartesian product

$$t = \{(1, 1), (2, 4), (3, 9), (4, 16), (5, 25)\}.$$

We can shortcut the maplet notation for a sequence by listing the objects in the sequence between angled brakets in the specific order required e.g. sequence t above can be written $\langle 1, 4, 9, 16, 25 \rangle$.

In the same way s, a sequence of type seq A in Fig. 8.1 can be written

$$\langle Monday, Tuesday, Wednesday, Thursday, Friday, Saturday, Monday \rangle.$$

In **Z**, sn gives the nth member of a sequence so that $t5$ is 25 (the value of the fifth member of the sequence t), while $s3$ is *Wednesday*. The empty sequence is an alternative notation to the empty function and is written as:

$$\langle\rangle = \{\} = \varnothing$$

We should note that the expression above is correctly typed because the type of the empty sequence is still $\mathbb{P}(\mathbb{N} \times A)$.

8.5 Formal definition of a sequence

The formal definition of a sequence of objects of type A is:

$$\text{seq } A == \{\, f : \mathbb{N} \nrightarrow A \mid \text{dom} f\, = 1..\#f\, \}$$

The set of finite sequences of objects of type A is declared as the set of partial finite functions f from the set of natural numbers   to A where n is a number such that the domain of f is the set of numbers from 1 to n inclusive, from the set of natural numbers. There cannot be any spaces in the sequence, the sequence goes from 1 to n and there will be n maplets.

8.6 Different kinds of sequences

We will now define some special kinds of sequences which are useful in applications.

Firstly, $seq_1 A$ represents the set of non-empty sequences over the set A, excluding the empty sequence:

$$\text{seq}_1 A = \text{seq } A \setminus \{\langle\rangle\}$$

An **injective sequence** is a set of sequences with no repetitions. For example, a queue of any kind would normally be expected to be a sequence with every member of A occupying only one place. iseq A is the set of injective sequences over A defined as:

$$\text{iseq } A == \text{seq } A \cap (\mathbb{N} \rightarrowtail A)$$

where $\mathbb{N} \rightarrowtail A$ is a partial finite injection from the set of natural numbers to A. These are finite sequences over A which contain no repetitions.

The length of a sequence is the number of elements in a sequence i.e. the number of maplets in the sequence function. The cardinality of the set of maplets #s denotes the length of sequence s.

8.7 Operations on sequences

Since sequences are important in most specifications, **Z** has evolved a set of special operators which can be used with them.

Every sequence has a head and a tail. The head of a sequence is the first member of the sequence and last is the last element in a sequence. The remaining elements without the head form a sequence called the tail. The front of a sequence is a sequence created be the removal of the last element. Therefore for sequence s

head s   denotes the first member of the sequence
tail s   denotes all the elements in a sequence except the first member
last s   is the last element in a sequence
front s   is the remaining elements of the sequence except the last member

Concatenation is the operation of forming a new sequence by joining two sequences in the correct order. Concatenation is shown by the $\frown$ symbol. Thus the head of an old sequence and the tail can be concatenated to give the original sequence.

$$s = (front \; s) \frown \langle last \; s\rangle$$
$$s = \langle head \; s \rangle \frown (tail \; s)$$

Note the use of angled brackets with head and last to make these into sequences. Concatenation is only valid with sequences.

Finally the sequence can be reversed so that the result is a sequence of the same elements but in the reverse order.

rev *s*   denotes the sequence which is the reverse of *s*.

We can then list the following relationships :

$$rev \langle \rangle = \langle \rangle$$
$$rev \langle x \rangle = \langle x \rangle$$
$$rev \, (rev \, s) = s$$

It is important to note that *head, tail, last* and *front* are operations which are not defined for the empty sequence. The operators *front, last, head* and *tail* can be used as we have seen above to break up a sequence. This is known as sequence **decomposition.**

Sequences are functions which are often convenient to define by induction (see section 8.2). Any sequence can be obtained from any empty sequence by repeatedly adding a new member. We can illustrate this by showing that some property P(s) holds for all finite sequences s: seq X because:

1) P(0) holds

2) If P(s) holds for some sequence s then P($s \frown \langle x \rangle$) also holds .

In this way the sequence can be built up by adding new members to the end of the sequence:

$$\forall s : \text{seq } X \, ; x : X \bullet \text{P}(s) \Rightarrow \text{P} (s \frown \langle x \rangle)$$

Exercise 1
Given that s :seq A $A == \{m, n, o, p, q, r\}$
      $s = \langle m, n, o, p, q, r \rangle$

What are the following ?
(1) *head s*
(2) *tail s*
(3) *tail* $\langle m \rangle$
(4) *front* s
(5) *last s*
(6) *front* $\langle p \rangle$
(7) *last* $\langle q \rangle$
(8) *rev   s*
(9)Use induction to define a sequence which
(a) grows from the front   instead of building up the end of the sequence
(b) grows from any position

8.8   Selecting from sequences

This is a process of selecting certain members of a sequence to produce a new sequence. The selection is carried out by matching a given set A to a sequence s. The **filtering** operation is shown by the $\upharpoonright$ symbol, for example, $s \upharpoonright A$ describes the sequence s filtered by the set A.

Example 5
Suppose the sequence of students ordered by their examination results is

$$\langle Fatima, Tim, Andrea, John, Lisa, Desmond \rangle$$

and A is the set of females $\{Andrea, Fatima, Lisa\}$.

If we wanted to get the female students in order of their examination results we would filter the sequence as follows :

$$s \upharpoonright A \; = \; \langle Fatima, Andrea, Lisa \rangle$$

Alternatively if we have a set B of male students $\{ Desmond, John, Tim\}$ we can filter the male students from the sequence s in the order of their examination results e.g.

$$s \upharpoonright B = \langle Tim, John, Desmond \rangle$$

Sometimes we will want to select from a sequence on the basis of the position of the items in the sequence. This can be carried out by the **extraction operator**, shown by the symbol $\upharpoonleft$.

Suppose we need the second, third and fifth members and we have a set of indices to the student sequence given by the set of indices U

$$U = \{ 2, 3, 5\}$$

We can extract the elements corresponding to these indices as follows:

$$U \upharpoonleft s = \; \langle Tim, Fatima, Lisa \rangle$$

Another useful selection operation is carried out by the function *squash* which creates a sequence from a partial finite function. This is illustrated in Fig. 8.2 below which shows the effects of the *squash* function on a finite function f.

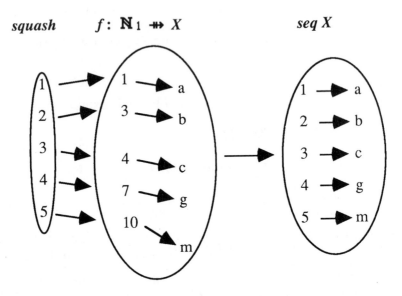

Fig. 8.2 The *squash* function

The *squash* function works by compacting a finite function which must be defined on strictly positive integers. The composition of a function *f* is with a special function whose domain consists of natural numbers from 1 to #*f* and whose range is the domain of *f*. In Fig. 8.2 although the function *f* has five maplets initially spaced from values 1 to 10 of the domain. After the *squash* operation a sequence is produced with no gaps.

In the second example below the squash function transforms the finite function *Marks* which maps students' marks to their names into a sequence in order of their results.

Example 6

Marks : $\mathbb{N} \twoheadrightarrow$ *Names*

Marks == {52 ↦ *Desmond*, 65 ↦ *Lisa*, 72 ↦ *John*, 81 ↦ *Andrea*,
    83 ↦ *Tim* , 95 ↦ *Fatima*}

The *squash* function can be applied as the finite partial function, *Marks*, is based on positive integers representing the marks from 1 to 100. The result of the *squash* function would be the following sequence:

squash (*Marks*) = ⟨*Desmond, Lisa, John, Andrea, Tim, Fatima*⟩

This is illustrated in detail in Fig. 8.3 below.

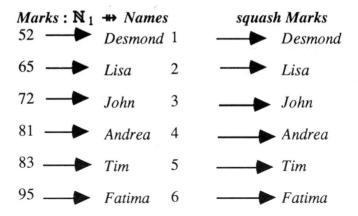

Fig. 8.3 Example of the squash function

It is clear now, that filtration and extraction are both particular applications of the *squash* function. Filtration is the equivalent to *squash* with domain restriction e.g.

$$s \upharpoonright A = squash\ (s \lhd A)$$

While extraction is the equivalent of *squash* function with range restriction.

$$U \upharpoonright s = squash\ (U \rhd s)$$

There is also another group of relations which can be applied to produce a selection from a sequence in the case when one sequence forms part of another sequence. When we want to identify a sequence as the begining of another sequence we can write :

$$s \textbf{ prefix } t$$

In the same way there is a relation **suffix** for the back of another sequence and a relation **in** to describe an arrangement where a sequence is found anywhere within a second longer sequence. These are denoted respectively as follows :

$$s \textbf{ suffix } t$$

$$s \textbf{ in } t$$

In each case the smaller sequence must form a **contiguous** part of the larger sequence. These relations can be identified with the filter and extraction functions above so that if we have two sequences s and t we see that :

$$s \text{ prefix } t \Leftrightarrow s = (1.. \#s)\mathbin{1} t$$

because prefix is the equivalent to an extraction from the front of a sequence. In the same way we see that, where u is any subset of s

$$s \text{ in } t \Leftrightarrow (\exists u : \text{seq } X \bullet s \text{ suffix } u \wedge u \text{ prefix } t)$$

the **in** operation is the combination of prefix and suffix operating together.

Example 7
We can apply these relations to our example of students' examination results. If we have the following sequences:

$$r = \langle Lisa, Desmond \rangle$$
$$s = \langle Andrea, Tim \rangle$$
$$t = \langle Andrea, Tim, Fatima, John, Lisa, Desmond \rangle$$
$$v = \langle Fatima, John \rangle$$
$$u = \langle Andrea, Tim, Fatima, John \rangle$$

We can write:

$$s \text{ prefix } t$$
$$r \text{ suffix } t$$
$$v \text{ in } t$$
$$\langle Fatima, John \rangle \text{ in } t \Leftrightarrow (v \text{ suffix } u \wedge u \text{ prefix } t)$$

It is possible to carry out an operation called **distributed concatenation** with sequences. This operation will link together a series of sequences of the same type to form a complete sequence. It is denoted by the symbol $\frown/$. For example, in the sequences above we can perform distributed concatenation on the sequences r, s and v to produce sequence t.

$$t = ((s \frown v) \frown r) = \langle Andrea, Tim, Fatima, John, Lisa, Desmond \rangle$$

In this case, we can see that t is the sequence of the sequences s, v, and r. We could write :

$$t = \frown/ \langle s, v, r \rangle$$

All the sequences in the concatenated sequence must be of the same type.

A related concept is **disjointness.** We may form a sequence of sets and say the sequence is disjoint when the intersection of all the sets is the empty set and no two sets in the sequence have any members in common. As an illustration of this concept the sequence w, below, is a sequence of disjoint sets:

$w = \langle \{Andrea, Tim\}, \{Fatima\}, \{John, Lisa, Desmond\} \rangle$

while the following example is not disjoint.

$\langle \{T, h, i, s\}, \{s, e, q, u, e, n, c, e\}, \{i, s\}, \{n, o, t\}, \{d, i, s, j, o, i, n, t\} \rangle$

In many applications it is useful to partition a collection of objects into several disjoint sets. For example, if the range of the disjoint sequence of students w above contained all the members of the set *Student*, the sequence would be said to have partitioned the set. This is denoted in **Z** by using the term **partition** and would be expressed as follows:

w **partition** *Student*

8.9 Relational operations on sequences

Sequences are special functions so that they are also special relations. Therefore it is possible to apply relational and functional operations to sequences.

A particularly useful operation is the use of **ran** to locate a set of members in a sequence. The range ran s of a sequence s is the set of elements which combine to form a sequence and the following relationships hold:

$$\text{ran} \langle x \rangle = \{x\}$$
$$\text{ran} \langle \, \rangle = \varnothing$$
$$\text{ran} (s \cap t) = (\text{ran } s) \cup (\text{ran } t)$$
$$\text{ran} (s \upharpoonright V) = (\text{ran } s) \cap V$$
$$\text{ran} (rev\ s) = \text{ran } s$$

Relational composition is also valid for sequences. It is possible to compose a sequence s with a function f to produce a new sequence based on the range of the function.

If $s : \text{seq } X$ and $f : X \to Y$ then $f \circ s \in \text{seq } Y$

The new sequence $f \circ s$ will be the same length as the original sequence s but the elments of the new sequence will be the images of the corresponding elements of s under f.

We can formalise the above statements by writing

$$\#(f \circ s) = \#s$$
$$\forall i : 1 .. \#s\ (f \circ s)(i) = f(s(i))$$

We find an interesting set of results from the composition of functions with sequences. For example:

$$f \circ \langle \, \rangle = \langle \, \rangle$$
$$f \circ \langle x \rangle = \langle f(x) \rangle$$

If we have a sequence s of type seq X then the type of the range of the sequence is the set X. If there is also a finite function

$$f : X \to Y$$

then this function can be composed with the original sequence s to form the new sequence of type seq Y. The next example will illustrate this process.

Example 9
A laboratory has records of blood sugar levels for patients. These are produced as a sequence ranked from the highest to the lowest for a set of anonymous samples as follows:

$$s = \langle 180, 140, 120, 100, 80 \rangle$$

The laboratory also has records showing the following function from blood sample level to patient:

$$f : X \to Y \ == \ \{(100, Chris), (180, Mike), (140, Frazer), (120, Andy), (80, Alan)\}$$

The composition of the function f with s gives the new sequence t which gives a sequence of the patients in the order of their blood sugar levels:

$$t = f \circ s \ = \langle Mike, Frazer, Andy, Chris, Alan \rangle$$

8.10 Sequences in an application

This section describes two different applications of sequences. The first is in music and the second example applies sequences to an employee database.

8.10.1 Music application

In music the notes of the music scale are named after the first seven letters of the alphabet, that is: A, B, C, D, E, F, G .

$$Scale == \{A, B, C, D, E, F, G \}$$

Different melodies are formed by creating different sequences of notes. The type of all the melodies is seq *Scale*. For example the beginning of *'Auld Lang Syne'* follows the sequence:

$Als = \langle A, D, D, D, F, E, D, E, F, D, D, F, A \rangle$

From an examination of the sequence we can see that two members of the set *Scale* do not appear in the sequence at all i.e. *B, C, G*. Some members are repeated many times e.g. there are five *D* notes. We can apply the sequence operators to decompose the theme of *' Auld Lang Syne '* as follows:

$Als = \langle A, D, D, D, F, E, D, E, F, D, D, F, A \rangle$
$head\ Als = A$
$tail\ Als = Als = \langle D, D, D, F, E, D, E, F, D, D, F, A \rangle$
$last\ Als = F$
$\{7 \mapsto D\} \in Als$
$\{8 \mapsto B\} \notin Als$

One of the themes for Dvorak's *'New World Symphony'* corresponds to the sequence:

$\langle C, E, E, C, B, A, B, C, D, C \rangle$

The underlying set *Scale* is still based on seven notes but the arrangement of the sequence creates a different melody. Many different melodies and phrases can be created from the same basic set. If the order of the sequence is changed the meaning of the sequence and the information conveyed is also changed. It may be noted that many electronic music generators are referred to as sequencers, since they produce sequences like these.

8.10.2 Employee database

This introduces the employee data file. The data file structure of *Employee* corresponds to a sequence of attributes:

Employee

empno	ename	dept
960	Jones	Finance
965	Smith	Computing
968	Johnson	Production
970	North	Finance
975	Williams	Computing

where:

empno: set of unique employee numbers
ename: set of employee names
dept :   set of department names, an employee can only belong to one
department and all employees belong to existing departments.

We will begin be defining the given types [*NAME* , *DEPT*]. We will
describe *Employee* as a schema type as follows:

```
┌─Employee────────────
│ empno : N
│ ename : NAME
│
└─────────────────────
```

The next schema, *Organisation*, describes the organisation of
employees into departments:

```
┌─Organisation────────────
│ worksin : Employee ⇸ DEPT
│
└─────────────────────────
```

Notice the use of the surjective function *worksin* to ensure that every
department has employees. The company has introduced a
performance appraisal system for all employees so that every member
of *Employee* has been ranked according to their performance. Some
employees have the same rank number. The rankings are modelled by
the use of a sequence called *perf* which is of type

perf : *seq Employee*

The employees are categorised as follows:

the top 20 employees are described as '*tops*' and get the highest bonus;
the next 50 employees are described as '*mids*' and get the average
bonus; the rest of the employees are described as '*poor*' and get the
lowest bonus.

We can express these arrangements formally through the use of
sequences and an index to the set *Employee* called *U*. *U* is distributed
into three sections U_1, U_2, U_3.

$U = \ ^\frown / \ \langle U_1, U_2, U_3 \ \rangle$
U_1 prefix $U \ \wedge \ \# U_1 = 20$ $tops = U_1 \ \upharpoonleft \ perf$
U_2 in $U \ \wedge \# U_2 = 50$ $mids = U_2 \ \upharpoonleft \ perf$
U_3 suffix $U \ \wedge \# U_3 = \# U\text{-}70$ $poor = U_3 \ \upharpoonleft \ perf$

and this resulted in splitting up the sequence *perf*

$perf =$ $\frown / \langle$ top , $mids$, $poor \rangle$
$\langle$ran (top), ran ($mids$), ran ($poor$) $\rangle$ partitions $Employee$

If the Head of the Computing department want to know the order of rankings of all the employees who work in '$Computing$ ' we can use range restriction of the function $worksin$ to give the computing details and then use dom to give a subset of $Employee$. In the example below the subset is called $compemp$ and is used to filter the sequence $perf$.

$compemp = $ dom ($worksn$ $\rhd$ $\{Computing\}$)

$answer = perf \restriction compemp = \langle(975, Williams), (968, Johnson)\rangle$

8.11 Summary

This chapter introduced two concepts which are important in developing specifications in **Z** - finite functions and sequences. The concepts used are built on the definition of functions found in chapter 3. Sequences were introduced as a means of describing ordered arrangements of objects such as lists. These lists could contain duplicate objects.

Sequences can be described and manipulated in **Z** through various operations. In particular sequences can be reversed, joined, subdivided and extracted. The keywords and symbols introduced in this chapter are summarised below:

$\mathbb{F}X$	represents a finite subset of $\mathbb{P}X$
$X \nrightarrow Y$	represents finite partial functions between X and Y
$X \rightarrowtail\mkern-14mu\rightarrow Y$	represents finite partial injections
$s : \mathbb{N} \rightarrow A$	represents the type of a sequence s of any set A
$s : $ seq A	represents sequence s of type seq A
$\langle a , b , c , ... \rangle$	represents a sequence of the elements of s
$\langle\rangle = \{ \} = \emptyset$	represents the empty sequence
ran s	the set of objects forming a sequence s
$seq_1 A$	represents the sets of non-empty sequences of the elements of A
iseq A	the set of injective sequences with no repetitions
rev s	denotes the sequence which is the reverse of s.

decomposition

$head$ s	denotes the first member of the sequence s
$tail$ s	denotes all the elements, except the first member.
$last$ s	the last element in a sequence s
$front$ s	the elements of the sequence except the last member

concatenation

⌢

represents concatenation, forming a new sequence by joining two sequences in the correct order

⌢/

distributed concatenation, link together a series of sequences of the same type

selection

$s \upharpoonright A$

filtering a sequence by a set A

squash f

compaction of finite function into a sequence

$U \upharpoonright s$

extraction of elements of an index U from a sequence

s prefix t

extraction from the front of a sequence

s suffix t

extraction from the back of a sequence

s in t

extraction where a sequence is found within a second longer sequence, combination of prefix and suffix

Exercise 2

(1) Chinese astrology is based on the animal ruling the year in which a person is born having a profound influence over life. The twelve signs can be represented by the set, *Sign*:

{*Rat, Ox, Tiger, Rabbit, Dragon, Snake, Horse, Sheep, Monkey, Rooster, Dog, Boar*}

The signs are further divided and called *Yin* and *Yang* respectively.

The *Yin* quality:{*Rat, Ox, Rabbit, Monkey, Dog, Boar*}

The *Yang* quality:{*Tiger, Dragon, Snake, Horse, Sheep, Rooster*}

In Example 9, the patients sequence of blood sugar levels were:

$t = \langle$ *Mike, Frazer, Andy, Chris, Alan* $\rangle$

Their Chinese signs are given by the function *Fate* as follows:

{*Mike* ↦ *Horse, Frazer* ↦ *Tiger, Andy* ↦ *Dragon , Chris* ↦ *Rooster, Alan* ↦ *Sheep*}

Use **Z** sequence notation to:

(a) Rearrange the people in the order of their Chinese signs.

(b) Identify the first and last member of the new sequence

(c) Give the *Yin* members of the group in their new sequence order

(d) Give the *Yang* members of the group in their new sequence order

(2) A service company keeps a list of customer arrival times and waiting times for its quality control system. Some of the data collected is shown below:

Customer	Service Point	Arrival Time	Service Time
A	1	1	10
B	2	1	5
C	2	2	6
D	1	3	7
E	1	6	5

Use **Z** functions and sequence notation to express

(1) the order of the customers at each service point

(2) the order of service times at each service point

9

Introduction to Bags

9.1 Introduction

This chapter introduces the concept of bags and the operations available in **Z** to model and manipulate bags of objects. The purpose behind the concept of a bag is to model a collection of repeated objects in a way which could not be achieved by using simple set theory.   Many specifications involve collections of objects with the same names. One could look upon a bag as a set of sets or a multi-set. In a stock control system there will be many items of stock with the same part name and identification number. In a book shop there may be many copies of books with the same titles and *ISBN* numbers. Care needs to be taken when modelling this type of application by means of sets since, strictly speaking, sets do not permit the repetition of objects. It is possible to solve some of these difficulties by using bags which are specialised collections of objects consisting of a list of the objects together with the frequency of occurrence of each object.

At the end of this chapter the reader should:

♦ understand the basic concepts of bags

♦ be able to apply various operations to bags

♦ understand the application of bags to simple models

♦ be able to formalise the use of bags in simple specifications

9.2 Basic concept

A bag is a specialised collection of objects modelled by using an ordered pair, which combines the name of an object from a particular set with the frequency of occurence of that object in the collection. All the objects in the bag must be of the same type.

This is illustrated in the following example.

Example 1

Suppose in a pocket there is a collection of coins corresponding to the denominations of 1p, 2p and 5p. The money in the pocket can be modelled by a bag. The pocket is found to contain four 1p coins, seven 2p coins and five 5p coins.

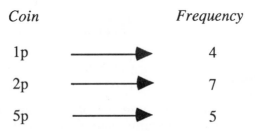

Fig. 9.1 Money in a bag

As we can see when we consider Fig. 9.1 a bag can be modelled by using a partial function from a set of objects, in this case from the set *Coin* to N_1.

We therefore define a bag as a partial function from a type A to N_1.

bag $A == A \nrightarrow N_1$

In **Z** bag A is a type which is declared as all the possible bags of type A. For example, the bag a formed from the set A is declared as follows:

a : bag A

Bags are shown by listing the members between special open square brackets. For example the bag notation $[\![a, a, a, a, b, b, c, c, c]\!]$ corresponds to the function $\{a \mapsto 4, b \mapsto 2, c \mapsto 3\}$. A bag $[\![a, b, b, c]\!]$ which is a collection of four objects is not the same as a set $\{a, b, c\}$ which consists of three objects only. The bag $[\![a, b, c]\!]$ contains three objects while the bag $[\![a, b, b, c]\!]$ contains four objects even though two of these have the same name, b.

There is no concept of order in the way in which objects are arranged in a bag. The bag $[\![a, b, b, c]\!]$ is the same as the bag $[\![a, b, c, b]\!]$. The empty bag is represented by the symbol $[\![\ ]\!]$ and is equivalent to the empty function.

bag A denotes the set of all the possible bags of the elements of the set A. If a set A is $\{a, b, c\}$ then bag A will denote the set of all the possible bags that could be made up from the set A, for example, including

$\{\ [\![a,\ b,\ b,\ c,\ c]\!]\ ,\ [\![a,\ a,\ a,\ b,\ c,]\!]\ ,\ [\![a,\ b,\ b,\ c,\ c,\ c]\!]\ ...\ \}$

9.3 Operations on bags

One of the reasons bags are very useful for modelling specifications where there are multiple occurences of objects with the same name is that a special collection of bag operations has been incorporated into the **Z** language.

Example 2
In a sales order from a D-I-Y shop, we may find the following information recorded

Sales Order

Salesitem	Quantity	Price	Line Total
Paint	3	£ 2.00	£ 6.00
Exotic wallpaper roll	2	£ 3.00	£ 6.00
Brush	1	£ 4.00	£ 4.00
		Total	£16.00

In this case we have a set of items {*paint, wallpaper, brush* } but the buyer has selected different numbers of each item which are given in one particular example of a bag called *Salesitems*.

$Salesitems\ ==\ \{paint \mapsto 3,\ wallpaper \mapsto 2,\ brush \mapsto 1\}$

It is possible by using bag operations and bag arithmetic to keep a check on the number of items ordered and also what is left in stock .

The following operations can be carried out on bags of the same type:

a) **bag membership.**
We use the operator $\sqsubseteq$ to check the membership of a bag and to find out whether a particular object is in the bag . We can write

$x \sqsubseteq B$

to represent object x in bag B. This is a predicate which is true if x is in the bag B and it appears a non-zero number of times. dom B is the domain of the partial function ,

$\text{bag } B\ ==B\ \nrightarrow \mathbb{N}_1$

and gives the actual elements of set B which are in the bag.

In the example of the Sales Order above, if S is a bag for this particular sales order of type bag B we can write, $brush \in S$ and $wallpaper \in S$. For example:

dom S = {$paint, wallpaper, brush$}

b) **sub-bag relation.**
A bag may be the sub-bag of another bag in the same way that a set can be a sub-set of another set. A bag B can be a sub-bag of another bag C of the same type, if each element in B occurs in B no more often than it occurs in C.

The symbol used to represent the sub-bag relation is $\sqsubseteq$ and we can write the relationship between bags, B and C, of the same type as follows:

$B \sqsubseteq C$

The domain of B must be a subset of the domain of C :

$B \sqsubseteq C \Rightarrow$ dom $B \subseteq$ dom C

The empty bag $[\![\,]\!]$ is a sub-bag of every other bag.

In Example 2, in the sales order, the items ordered must be available in stock, so that the bag of sales items must be a sub-bag of the bag of stock.

bag $Items$ == $Items \nrightarrow \mathbb{N}_1$

$\forall Salesitems, stock$: bag $Items$ • $Salesitems \sqsubseteq stock$.

c) **counting objects in bags.**
count B x represents the number of times x appears in a bag, B .

In the sales order bag $Salesitems$, it can be seen that

count $Salesitems$ $brush$ = 1
count $Salesitems$ $wallpaper$ = 2
count $Salesitems$ $paint$ = 3

d) **bag union**
This is the joining of two bags of the same type together and is represented by the special symbol $\uplus$ so that $B \uplus C$ gives a new bag made up of the objects in the bags B and C. The domain of the new bag will be the result of the union of the domains of the separate bags.

dom $(B \uplus C) = $ dom $B \cup$ dom C

count $(B \uplus C)x = count\ B\ x + count\ C\ x$

For example, suppose we have the following bags A, B and C of the same type so that we can perform bag arithmetic upon them :

$A == \{a \mapsto 1, b \mapsto 2\}$
$B == \{a \mapsto 3, b \mapsto 6\}$
$C == \{a \mapsto 3, b \mapsto 6, c \mapsto 4\}$

The union of bags A and B will give

$A \uplus B = \{a \mapsto 4, b \mapsto 8\}$

The bag union operator is commutative just like normal addition so that we can write

$B \uplus A = \{a \mapsto 4, b \mapsto 8\}$

In the same way it is possible to add all three bags together :

$(A \uplus B) \uplus C = \{a \mapsto 4, b \mapsto 8\} \uplus \{a \mapsto 3, b \mapsto 6, c \mapsto 4\}$
$= \{a \mapsto 7, b \mapsto 14, c \mapsto 4\}$

The same result will arise whether we add the bags together in any order.

$A \uplus (B \uplus C) = \{a \mapsto 1, b \mapsto 2\} \uplus \{a \mapsto 6, b \mapsto 12, c \mapsto 4\}$
$= \{a \mapsto 7, b \mapsto 14, c \mapsto 4\}$

It will always be the case that when we carry out bag union we get the following result :

$(A \uplus B) \uplus C = A \uplus (B \uplus C)$

d) **Bag difference.**
The bag difference of two bags B and C which must be of the same type, will operate on every element in the bag B to take away the number of times an object appears in bag C . If, for any object in the bag, the result of the bag difference operation would be a negative number, this becomes zero because it is not possible to have a negative frequency. The bag difference is represented by the symbol

⊎. For the bags above, A and B, we can declare the difference between bag B and A as follows :

$$B \uplus A = \{a \mapsto 2, b \mapsto 4\}$$

The bag difference operator is not commutative because if we ask for the difference between A and B we get a different result :

$$A \uplus B = \{a \mapsto 0, b \mapsto 0\} = [\![\,]\!]$$

In this way we can obtain an empty bag.

The effect of using an empty bag with the bag difference operator needs to be noted carefully.

$$A \uplus [\![\,]\!] = A$$
$$[\![\,]\!] \uplus A = [\![\,]\!]$$

The difference between the bag of stock and the bag of the sales order will give the stock available for sale. We can write in **Z** notation

$stock' = stock \ \uplus \ Salesitems$

f) There is a final operator for **scaling bags** which is represented by the symbol ⊗. A bag can be scaled by a natural number so that we can write $n \otimes A$ to represent the bag, A, scaled by the factor n. The result will be another bag where any element appears in the new bag n times as often as it appears in the bag, A. For example:

$$A == \{a \mapsto 1, b \mapsto 2\}$$
$$3 \otimes A = 3 \otimes \{a \mapsto 1, b \mapsto 2\} = \{a \mapsto 3, b \mapsto 6\}$$

$$B == \{a \mapsto 2, b \mapsto 3\}$$
$$3 \otimes B = 3 \otimes \{a \mapsto 2, b \mapsto 3\} = \{a \mapsto 6, b \mapsto 9\}$$

It is important to note that when any bag is scaled by the factor 0, the result will be the empty bag :

$$0 \otimes A = [\![\,]\!]$$

and when the empty bag is scaled the result is still the empty bag:

$$3 \otimes [\![\,]\!] = [\![\,]\!]$$

It is possible to combine scaling with bag union so that we can see that

$$3 \otimes (A \uplus B) = 3 \otimes \{a \mapsto 3, b \mapsto 5\} = \{a \mapsto 9, b \mapsto 15\}$$

This is the same result as if we combined our previous results

$$3 \otimes A \uplus 3 \otimes B = \{a \mapsto 9, b \mapsto 15\}$$

These results are both examples of a general law

$$3 \otimes (A \uplus B) = 3 \otimes A \uplus 3 \otimes B$$

$$n \otimes (A \uplus B) = n \otimes A \uplus n \otimes B$$

Example 4
The menu items for a buffet lunch for   members of a working group in an organisation can consist of the following items:

Menu == { *sandwich, pizza, quiche, apple, savoury* }

The lunch for each person can be modelled by using a bag which we will call *lunch* of the type bag *Menu*. The result will be:

lunch = {*sandwich* ↦ 3, *quiche* ↦ 2, *apple* ↦ 1, *savoury* ↦ 2 }

We can use the bag scaling operator to find out the quantities ordered for a meeting of twelve.

12 ⊗ *lunch* = {*sandwich* ↦ 36, *quiche* ↦ 24, *apple* ↦ 12, *savoury* ↦ 24}

Bag scaling can be combined with bag difference to perform powerful arithmetic on bags.

Example 5
This example looks at the stock levels of items which we will call *a*, *b*, and *c* of the set *stockitems*.

stockitems == {*a*, *b*, *c*}

The stock levels for each item are shown by using a bag called *stock* of type bag *stockitems*.

stock = {*a* ↦ 20, *b* ↦ 40, *c* ↦ 30}

A standard pack of a, b, and c is available for sale. The pack is represented by the bag *standard* which is the same type as *stock*.

standard $= \{a \mapsto 2, b \mapsto 1, c \mapsto 3\}$

A bulk buy pack is available which is five times the size of a standard pack.

bulk $= 5 \otimes$ *standard*

The available stock after each sale of the bulk pack will be

stock' $=$ *stock* $\uplus$ $(5 \otimes$ *standard* $)$

Exercise 1
Given the two bags, A and B , of the same type :

$A = \{l \mapsto 4, m \mapsto 3, n \mapsto 5\}$
$B = \{l \mapsto 2, m \mapsto 2, n \mapsto 3\}$

What are the following :

(a) *count A m*

(b) *count B m*

(c) $A \uplus B$

(d) $A \uplus B$

(e) $4 \otimes A$

(f) *count* $(4 \otimes A)$ *n*

(g) *count* $(0 \otimes A)$ *l*

(h) show that $B \sqsubseteq A$

9.4 Bags and sequences

Both bags and sequences deal with multiple copies of objects with the same names. A sequence is an ordered list of objects which can include repetition, since an object can appear any number of times in the list. In many cases a systems specification may include the need to know how many times an object occurs in a sequence. A sequence can be turned into a bag of the same objects which make up the sequence by using the operator *items*.

If s is a sequence, *items* s is the bag in which each element x in the bag appears exactly as often as x appears in the sequence s. As an illustration consider sales of drinks from a vending machine which have been recorded in the following sequence:

$s = \langle$ *cola, lemon, orange, cola, cola, lemon, orange, cola, cola* $\rangle$

It will be important to know how many of each type of drink has been sold. *items* will turn the sequence into a bag

items s = ⟦*cola, lemon, orange, cola, cola, lemon, orange, cola, cola*⟧

The bag operators can then provide the information :

> *count* (*items s*) *lemon* = 2
> *count* (*items s*) *cola* = 5

9.5 Bags in applications

Bags have many applications in systems where there is a need to model multiple copies of objects with the same name. Widely found examples are in stock control and in sales order processing. In a stock control system many copies of the same product will be stored and subsequently sold. Below is a typical stock record with the product identifier, Part Number, the quantity available for sale, and the re-order quantity :

Part Number	Quantity	Re-order Quantity
101	5	20
104	20	20
105	22	10
108	30	50
110	40	20

Fig. 9.2 Stock Record

The table above in Fig. 9.2, shows Quantity is a partial function of Part Number and could be modelled in this way. However we can also look upon the stock record as a bag of Part Numbers. The advantage of using a bag instead of developing our own function is that all the operators on bags, which we have studied in the above sections (9.2 and 9.3), are immediately available.

We will assume that the specification includes the basic type [*PART*] and that the parts are named by a sequence of three numbers from 100 to 999. We can define the bag of type *PART* as follows :

bag *PART* == *PART* $\nrightarrow \mathbb{N}_1$

The stock record table in Fig. 9.2 can be described by *stock* , a bag of type bag *PART* as follows :

stock = {101 $\mapsto$ 5, 104 $\mapsto$ 20, 105 $\mapsto$ 22, 108 $\mapsto$ 30, 110 $\mapsto$ 40}

The Re-order Quantity forms another bag, *Reord*, of the same type i.e. bag *PART*

$$Reord = \{101 \mapsto 20, 104 \mapsto 20, 105 \mapsto 10, 108 \mapsto 50, 110 \mapsto 20\}$$

When a customer places a sales order for one or more of these parts of type *PARTS* the customer order must show the part number selected and the quantity ordered.

Customer Order

Cusomer Name : Mr Smith   **Date :** 26/12/95

Part Number	Quantity	Price	Line Total
101	3	£ 2.00	£ 6.00
108	2	£ 3.00	£ 6.00
110	1	£ 4.00	£ 4.00
		Total	£16.00

Fig. 9.3 Customer Order

In Fig. 9.3 above we see another bag of the elements of the type *PART* but this time the quantity is the quantity ordered so that we will call the bag, *Ord* :

$$Ord = \{101 \mapsto 3, 108 \mapsto 2, 110 \mapsto 1\}$$

For the sales order to succeed the quantity ordered in the case of each part must be less than or equal to the quantity available. This means that the bag *Ord* must always be a subset of the bag *stock*.

$$Ord \sqsubseteq stock$$

These ideas can be expressed in two schemas which use the basic type [*PART*] as shown below:

```
┌──────stockholding ────────
│  stock  : bag PART
│  reord : bag PART
│─────────────────────────
│  dom reord ⊆ dom stock
└──────────────────────────
```

```
┌──────Sales───────────────
│ Ξ stockholding
│ price : PART ⇸ N₁
│ ord    : bag PART
├──────────────────────────
│ dom stock ⊆ dom price
│ ord ⊑ stock
└──────────────────────────
```

$$\text{price} : PART \nrightarrow \mathbb{N}_1$$
$$\text{ord} : \text{bag } PART$$
$$\text{dom } stock \subseteq \text{dom } price$$
$$\text{ord} \sqsubseteq stock$$

9.6 Summary

This chapter has show how **Z** deals with specification of multi-occurrences of objects through the use of bags, bag operations and bag arithmetic.

The main keywords used in this Chapter are summarised below:

BAG NOTATION

bag $A == A \nrightarrow \mathbb{N}_1$	the type of bag A
$[\![a, b, b, c, c, c]\!]$	represents elements within bag brackets.
$[\![\ ]\!]$	represents the empty bag
$\mathbb{E}$	bag membership.
$x \mathbb{E} B$	represents object x in bag, B
$\sqsubseteq$	sub-bag membership
$B \sqsubseteq C$	represents B as a sub-bag of C
$count\ A\ x$	will give the frequency of x in bag A
$A \uplus B$	represents the bag union of A with B
$A \uplus B$	represents the bag difference of B from A
$n \otimes A$	represents the bag scaling of A by factor n
$items\ s$	will turn the sequence, s into a bag

Laws

$$A \uplus [\![\ ]\!] = A$$
$$n \otimes (A \uplus B) = n \otimes A \uplus n \otimes B$$
$$\text{dom } (B \uplus C) = \text{dom } B \cup \text{dom } C.$$
$$count\ (B \uplus C)\ x = count\ Bx + count\ Cx$$

Exercise 2

(1) A table of students' examination results is as follows:

Student	Maths	Computing	French	Design
Fatima	95	67	56	59
Tim	83	85	47	49
Andrea	75	80	50	45
John	46	58	40	60
Lisa	45	60	55	48
Desmond	70	45	63	55

Using given types [STUDENT, SUBJECT], apply the concepts of sets and bags to the table of results above to:

(a) write expressions for the average mark of each student in all subjects
(b) write expressions for the average mark of all students in each subject

(2) The members of a local tennis league play doubles together. Four members play three matches of nine games each. In this way they take turns to play doubles together. The results are as follows:

Player	Match1	Match2	Match3	Total
Jenny	6	5	7	18
Maureen	6	4	2	12
Ros	3	4	7	14
Lynne	3	5	2	10

Use bags to model each match and player's results. Show how operations on bags can be used to give the overall results of each player and the answers to the following :

(a) the bags of games for Match1, Match2, Match3
(b) the total number of games won by Jenny
(c) the difference between the score of Ros in her first and last match
(d) the average score of Maureen in the three matches.

10

Further Z Examples

10.1 Introduction

Previous chapters have introduced a number of examples of Z schemas. These were principally in chapters 5 and 7. Using examples from our music library and related topics as illustrations, this chapter introduces the following points:

♦ a more complex schema to describe the loan of a recording

♦ a schema which describes a reservation of a recording which employs the predicate calculus

♦ simple examples of generic definitions

♦ a more complex example, *squash*, of a generic definition

♦ using generic definitions to describe the idea of a membership list and other lists

♦ using a related library, a video library, to illustrate the idea of generic schemas

♦ simple examples of schema normalisation

♦ schema normalisation applied to a music library example - emphasising the point that schema normalisation should take place whenever propositional connectives are used between schemas, particularly the negation operator and the equivalence and implication connectives

♦ schema types, bindings and the theta notation

10.2 A loan schema

Using the, by now, relatively familiar scenario of the music library we first write a schema to describe the making of a new loan. This example does not consider error conditions.

```
┌─MakeLoan ─────────────────────────────────┐
│ ΔMusicLib                                   │
│ mem?              : Person                  │
│ copyref?          : Copy                    │
├─────────────────────────────────────────────┤
│ mem?              ∈ member                  │
│ copyref?          ∈ dom held                │
│ copyref?          ∉ dom loan                │
│ loan'   = loan ∪ {copyref? ↦ mem?}          │
│ member'           = member                  │
│ held'             = held                    │
│ reservation'      = reservation             │
└─────────────────────────────────────────────┘
```

This schema starts by calling Δ*MusicLib* with all that has been previously mentioned in chapter 5 concerning the Δ convention. The schema then goes on to introduce a variable *mem?* as an input. This is the member who is making the loan. We then introduce the variable *copyref?* as another input variable, being the reference of the copy of the recording that is being borrowed.

There are three lines of preconditions in the predicate of this schema. The first insists that *mem?* is a member of the library, the second that the reference being used actually refers to a copy held by the library. The third precondition requires that the particular copy is not already out on loan to another member.

The remaining lines of the predicate for *MakeLoan* follow the usual pattern set by the schemas in chapter 5. The *loan* relation is increased by addition of the set containing the maplet *copyref?* ↦ *mem?*. The remaining lines show that no changes take place to any of the other variables during the course of making a new loan. Recall that these lines cannot be left out of a Δ schema.

10.3 A reservation schema

There is a further condition which we would like to impose on this music library. That is that we would want to ensure the very reasonable condition that reservations are only made for recordings of which all copies are out on loan. To do this we involve the predicate calculus, covered in chapter 6. The schema is written next and is followed by an explanation:

```
┌─MakeReservation ──────────────────────────────
│ ΔMusicLib
│ mem?              : Person
│ record?           : Recording
├────────────────────────────────────────────────
│ mem?              ∈ member
│ record?           ∈ ran held
│ ∀c :Copy | held(c) = record? • c ∈ dom loan
│ loan'             = loan
│ member'           = member
│ held'             = held
│ reservation'      = reservation ∪ {record? ↦ mem?}
└────────────────────────────────────────────────
```

This schema follows the familiar pattern, using Δ*MusicLib* as in previous schemas, together with the input variables *mem?* and *record?*. The predicate also follows the familiar pattern of previous chapters. There are firstly three precondition lines, then lines stating the relationship between the 'before' variables and the 'after' ones. The last line states that the new set *reservation'* will be made up of the old set *reservation* with the addition of the singleton set containing the maplet *record?* ↦ *mem?*. The only unfamiliar line is line 3 of the predicate part of the schema. Here, the universal quantifier is used to ensure that, for all copies which the library holds, where the copies are of the recording presented at the input (*record?*), then all these copies are out on loan.

It is interesting to note that if a request is made for a member to reserve a recording that s/he has already requested, this schema will not reject it, neither will it change the set of reservations. This is because, as mentioned in earlier chapters, a set with apparently two occurrences of the same element will in fact only contain one such occurrence.

10.4 Generic definitions

In any well ordered library system there exist alphabetic order lists of the objects involved in the library. Our music library is no exception. However, before creating these we need to introduce some more Z terminology, that of **generic definitions**.

A generic definition is very useful when we want to introduce an operation of some sort which could be applied to many different kinds of sets. As a simple example, we might want to find the first and second item in an ordered pair. We therefore write a generic definition to find these two items from any ordered pair. We define two generic operations, *first* and *second*, which appear below in a generic definition. This has the superficial appearance of a Z schema but it is not one. Note that it has double lines which form the upper boundary of the box. A description of the definition in natural language follows after the formal definition.

$$
\begin{array}{|l}
\hline\hline
[A, B] \\
first : A \times B \rightarrow A \\
second : A \times B \rightarrow B \\
\hline
(\forall x : A \; ; \; y : B \; \bullet \; first\,(x,y) = x \land second\,(x,y) = y) \\
\hline
\end{array}
$$

Here we have stated that both *first* and *second* are total functions from all ordered pairs of type $A \times B$ to the set A for *first* and to set B for *second*. These functions were first introduced in chapter 3. The reader will recall that when we apply *first* to the pair we retrieve the first element of that pair, and similarly for *second*. To illustrate the use of this concept, we consider an ordered pair:

$$name = (Jocasta\,,\,Brown)$$

We could thus find the surname of this person with the expression

second name

which evaluates to 'Brown'.

Looking again at our music library, we will expand on the idea from chapter 8 of the *squash* function and write it as a generic definition. We will then go on to define further generic definitions to help us achieve the objective of an alphabetic order of a membership list.

Considering first the *squash* function, this may be applied to partial functions in order to derive sequences. It is a useful concept when we have an initial sequence *aseq*, say, but wish to remove certain items from the list corresponding to those elements whose positions are the numbers in a certain set, *aset*, say. It is not enough to use domain subtraction and to write, for example:

$$\{aset\} \mathbin{\lhd\mkern-9mu-} aseq$$

This is because this would create a function which may no longer be a sequence, since its domain is no longer $1..n$ for some natural number n. It might have holes in it. The *squash* function provides us with the answer to this dilemma, and here follows its formal definition, a further example of a generic definition.

$=[X]$=================================

$squash : (\mathbb{N} \nrightarrow X) \nrightarrow \text{seq } X$

$(\forall fun : \mathbb{N} \nrightarrow X \mid (\exists num : \mathbb{N} \bullet (\forall m : \text{dom } fun \bullet num > m))$ **1.**
$\bullet ((fun = \varnothing \wedge squash\, fun = \langle \rangle)$ **2.**
$\vee (\exists least : \text{dom } fun \mid (\forall m : \text{dom } fun \bullet least \leq m)$ **3.**
$\bullet squash\, fun = \langle fun\, least \rangle \frown squash\, (\{least\} \lhd fun)))$ **4.**

Note that in this definition *squash* is not a total function. There is a universal quantifier below the line which has a constraint limiting the domain to those functions which are finite. The definition is recursive and in broad terms it states that the squash of a 'sequence with holes' is the same as the concatenation of the single element sequence that contains just the first member of the 'sequence with holes' with the squash of the remainder.

We now give a more detailed explanation of the *squash* definition, referring to the line numbers as indicated. Line 1 constrains the predicate to consider only partial finite functions.

Lines 3 and 4 state, firstly, that there is a number which can be found to be the smallest in the domain of the function, and, secondly, that the *squash* of the function is equal to the concatenation of this single element sequence, which contains just the element mapped by the smallest number, with the *squash* of the remainder of the function.

We can think of each step of the recursion (i.e. the definition *squash* calling up itself) as picking up elements from the function in question least first to form the new sequence until we have to *squash* an empty function.

Line 2 tells us that the *squash* of an empty function is an empty sequence and thus the recursion stops.

10.5 Library lists

Having now grasped the concept of generic definitions, we go on to introduce a new definition *inorder* to encapsulate what it means to have an alphabetic ordering between elements of a pair.

inorder is the set of all pairs of type *A*, such that the first element of the pair is earlier than the second.

```
┌═[A]══════════════════════════════════════
│ inorder : ℙ(A ↔ A)
├──────────────────────────────────────────
│ inorder = { _earlier_ : A ↔ A |
│        ∀l, m, n : A •
│          (l earlier m ∧ m earlier n ⇒ l earlier n)        1.
│        ∧ ( l earlier m ∧ m earlier l ⇒ l = m)             2.
│        ∧ ( l ≠m ⇒ l earlier m ∨ m earlier l)}             3.
└──────────────────────────────────────────
```

The alphabetic order as defined above needs certain properties as defined in its predicate. Firstly, from line 1 above, if an element *l* comes earlier in the ordering than *m*, and *m* is earlier than *n*, then *l* is earlier than *n*. Secondly, from line 3 above, provided that *l* and *m* are distinct, then either *l* is earlier than *m* or *m* is earlier than *l*.

Line 2 indicates that should we find that an *l* is earlier than an *m* and also that this *m* is earlier than the *l*, then the *l* is the same as the *m*.

The definition thus written states that for a given type, *A*, the set *inorder*[A] is the set of all alphabetically ordered relations with type $A ↔ A$.

We now go on and define a generic definition *placeinorder*, which takes a finite set and converts it into a sequence whose length is the size of the set, and which contains all the elements of the set in the given alphabetic order, as follows:

```
┌═[A]══════════════════════════════════════
│ placeinorder : (𝔽A × inorder[A]) → seq A
├──────────────────────────────────────────
│ placeinorder = { aset : 𝔽A ; anorder : inorder[A] ; aseq : seq A |
│     (#aseq = #aset ∧ aset = ran aseq                          1.
│     ∧ (∀p, q ∈ 1..#aset | p < q • (aseq p, aseq q) ∈ anorder))  2.
│     • ( aset, anorder) ↦ aseq}                                3.
└──────────────────────────────────────────
```

In the definition above, line1 ensures a) that the resultant sequence has the same number of elements as in the starting set and b) that no more and no less than the starting set makes up the range of the sequence.

Line 2 ensures that all pairs of elements in the sequence conform to the requirement that if the their first element's place number is less than their second's, then the first element's value is earlier in order than the second's.

Line 3 shows the form of a typical element of the resulting set.

In order to place any of the music library sets into ordered lists, we now merely have to apply the function *placeinorder* to what ever set we require. Thus an alphabetically ordered list of members of our music library would be written:

```
┌─MemberList ──────────────────────────────
│ ≡MusicLib
│ memlist! : seq Person
├──────────────────────────────────────────
│ memlist! = placeinorder (member, inorder [Person])
└──────────────────────────────────────────
```

10.6 Generic schemas

A further useful concept is that of **generic schemas**. These are used when identical operations are required to be performed on different set types. They are very similar to generic definitions except that they are true schemas. The following example shows a possible application of the concept to a problem related to our music library.

We might have a specification which is exactly parallel to the music library and which dealt with videos rather than music recordings. Further, for the sake of argument we might wish to write generic schemas which could operate on both libraries. Assume for these purposes that the video library has exactly the same structure as the music library. Its state invariant schema is called *VideoLib* and its basic types are [Person], [VideoCopy] and [VideoRecording] .We could write a generic enquiry schema where the formal types are referred to as *GCopy* and *GPerson*:

```
┌─GenericLoanEnquiry [GCopy, GPerson]──────
│ loanMap        : GCopy ⇸ GPerson
│ gcopyref?      : GCopy
│ gmem!          : GPerson
├──────────────────────────────────────────
│ gcopyref?      ∈ dom loanMap
│ gmem!          = loanMap(gcopyref?)
└──────────────────────────────────────────
```

This is very similar to the schema *WhoHasCopy* from chapter 5 section 5.14. For ease of comparison we reproduce the latter below:

```
┌─WhoHasCopy ──────────────────────
│  ΞMusicLib
│  copyref?              : Copy
│  mem!                  : Person
├──────────────────────────────────
│  copyref?              ∈ dom loan
│  mem!                  = loan(copyref?)
└──────────────────────────────────
```

As can be seen, the major difference is that the *WhoHasCopy* schema includes the Ξ*MusicLib* schema. However, when the *GenericLoanEnquiry* schema is called, it needs to quote the actual types under consideration which would take the place of the formal types *GCopy* and *GPerson*. In this respect students of programming will be reminded of parameter passing in Pascal procedures and 'C' language functions. The first line of the declaration section of *GenericLoanEnquiry* introduces a function, *loanMap*, which parallels the loan function in *MusicLib*. Thereafter the two schemas map each other exactly.

10.7 Schema normalisation - simple examples

The reader might recall a fleeting reference to schema normalisation in chapter 7, when we were discussing the negation operator. We now proceed to cover this topic more fully. We say that a schema is normalised when its declarations are given in their full form, or, in other words, in terms of their maximal types. When normalising we also have to make any consequent additions to the predicate. To give a very simple example we might have two schemas *Alpha* and *Beta* as follows:

```
┌─Alpha ───────────────────
│  aVariable         : ℕ₁
│  aGroup            : ℙ ℤ
├──────────────────────────
│  aVariable         ∈ aGroup
└──────────────────────────
```

```
┌─Beta ────────────────────
│  aVariable         : ℤ
│  bGroup            : ℙ ℤ
├──────────────────────────
│  aVariable         ∉ bGroup
└──────────────────────────
```

Here the types of *aVariable* in the schemas *Alpha* and *Beta* appear to be different, but their **maximal** types are both the same, namely $\mathbb{Z}$. In order to combine these two schemas with a propositional connective both schemas need to be in a normalised form. Clearly *Alpha* is not. Therefore we normalise it to:

```
┌─NormAlpha ────────────────────
│  aVariable        : ℤ
│  aGroup           : ℙ ℤ
├────────────────────────────────
│  aVariable        > 0
│  aVariable        ∈ aGroup
└
```

Thus, when we combine *Alpha* and *Beta* to make *Gamma*, say, as in:

$$Gamma \cong Alpha \Rightarrow Beta$$

we get an expanded version of *Gamma*:

```
┌─Gamma ─────────────────────────────
│  aVariable        : ℤ
│  aGroup, bGroup   : ℙ ℤ
├─────────────────────────────────────
│  (aVariable  > 0      ∧ aVariable  ∈ aGroup
│                       ⇒ aVariable  ∉ bGroup)
└
```

In the above we have replaced the non maximal set $\mathbb{N}_1$ by the maximal one $\mathbb{Z}$ and introduced the predicate statement that *aVariable* must be greater than zero. The combination of schemas with propositional connectives is only strictly valid when the schemas are normalised. As a further example we consider a very simple schema negation. If we had a schema which denoted a serial number, of one of the states of the USA, for example:

$$StateNum \cong [n : \mathbb{N}_1 \mid n \leq 50]$$

and we wished to negate it ¬ *StateNum,* we should be looking for a schema that produces a number that is **not** in the range 1..50. In other words, this number could be any negative number, zero, or any positive number which is greater than 50. If we simply negate the predicate part of *StateNum* we would get a schema:

$$PseudoNegStateNum \cong [n : \mathbb{N}_1 \mid n > 50]$$

As can be seen this excludes negative numbers and zero. In order to produce the correct result we need to normalise *StateNum* as:

$$StateNum \cong [n : \mathbb{Z} \mid n > 0 \wedge n \leq 50]$$

We can thus produce the correct $\neg StateNum$ as:

$$\neg StateNum \cong [n : \mathbb{Z} \mid n \leq 0 \vee n > 50]$$

10.8 Schema normalisation applied to the music library

For clarification purposes, this example uses schemas which have been broken down into smaller parts in order to get closer to the reasons for normalisation. Let us define an operation which removes a copy of a recording from our library as:

$$RemoveCopyFromStock \cong HeldInStock \wedge \neg OutOnLoan$$
$$\wedge TakeFromStock$$

In other words, in order to perform the operation, the recording must first actually be held by the music library and it must not be out on loan before we can take it from stock. We can write 'mini' schemas to describe these three states:

$$HeldInStock \cong [held : Copy \nrightarrow Recording ; copyref? : Copy \mid copyref? \in \text{dom } held\,]$$

$$OutOnLoan \cong [loan : Copy \nrightarrow Person ; copyref? : Copy \mid copyref? \in \text{dom } loan\,]$$

$$TakeFromStock \cong [\Delta MusicLib ; copyref? : Copy \mid held' = \{copyref?\} \lhd held\,]$$

As we can see, we have employed the negation operator in front of the *OutOnLoan* schema, and we have to make sure that we do this on a normalised schema. The normalised version of *OutOnLoan* is:

```
┌─NormalOutOnLoan ─────────────
│ loan:    : ℙ(Copy × Person)
│ copyref? : Copy
├──────────────────────────────
│ copyref? ∈ dom loan
│ loan    ∈ Copy ↠ Person
└──────────────────────────────
```

Here, we have ensured that the types are maximal types by writing $\mathbb{P}(Copy \times Person)$ as the type of *loan*. We then go on to constrain the values of *loan* to those we desire by the second line of predicate, $loan \in Copy \nrightarrow Person$. Thus the schema we require corresponding to $\neg OutOnLoan$ is *NotOutOnLoan*:

```
┌─NotOutOnLoan ──────────────
│ loan:    : ℙ(Copy × Person)
│ copyref?            : Copy
├─────────────────────────────
│ copyref? ∉ dom loan          ∨
│     loan ∉ Copy ↠ Person
└─────────────────────────────
```

The predicate for this schema has been produced using the well known equality from the propositional calculus(see exercise in Chapter 6):

$$\neg (p \wedge q) \Leftrightarrow \neg p \vee \neg q$$

We thus have a perhaps surprising outcome in that, not only does the *NotOutOnLoan* schema require the item requested not to be out on loan, but it also allows the alternative of *loan* not being a partial function. In other words by negating a schema we have introduced a possibly undesirable side effect. Only by explicitly writing it out can we see it. This demonstrates that negating schemas is not to be undertaken lightly. Side effects must be examined and taken into account. In our case the possibility that *loan* is not a function is immediately excluded again by conjoining the schema *NotOutOnLoan* with the schema *TakeFromStock*. This latter has embedded in it the ΔMusicLib schema, which contains the mandatory requirement that *loan* is a partial function.

10.9 Schema types

In order to illustrate the usage of schematypes we take examples from libraries in general. This naturally includes our music library. We state that we wish to write schemas which emphasise features concerning the members of a library. We therefore write the schema:

```
┌─Members ──────────────────
│ borrower, member : ℙ Person
├───────────────────────────
│ borrower         ⊆ member
│ #member          ≤ maxnum
└───────────────────────────
```

where *maxnum* is defined as the maximum number of members a library could manage. *Members* has now effectively been declared as a new type, a **schema type**. A schema type is an association between names and types. In determining the type of a schema it is the names in the declaration section of the schema which are important. The predicate section is ignored. Thus *Stuff* below declares the same type as *Members* even though the predicate section is not what we might desire.

```
┌─Stuff ──────────────────────────
│ borrower, member : ℙ Person
├──────────────────────────────────
│ borrower      ∩ member  = ∅
│ #borrower     ≤ #member
└──────────────────────────────────
```

Another way of writing the schema type *Members* is as follows:

$$⟨ borrower : ℙ Person ; member : ℙ Person ⟩$$

This notation is usually used when we wish to emphasise that a schema type includes all instances of the declared variables, even those that do not satisfy the predicate.

Now that *Members* has been declared as a type, it can be used in the declaration of further schemas, such as:

```
┌─TwoLibMems ─────────────────────
│ videoMembers, musicMembers : Members
└──────────────────────────────────
```

Here we have introduced two further sets, both of type *Members*, which describe some aspects of the members of a video library and a music library.

10.10 Selection

In the schema above, *TwoLibMems*, we have defined two libraries' members. We can now **select** components of these members by using a dot as:

$$musicMembers. borrower$$

This denotes the *borrowers* component of *musicMembers*. We can use the above to write a schema for some simple action on the library in question. Here we write a schema to describe in a very simple way the addition of a new member to a music library:

```
┌─MusicLibNewMem ────────────────────────────
│ ΔTwoLibMems
│ newmem?              : Person
├────────────────────────────────────────────
│ videoMembers'      = videoMembers
│ musicMembers'. borrower    = musicMembers. borrower
│ musicMembers'. member      =
│        musicMembers. member ∪ {newmem?}
└────────────────────────────────────────────
```

The above, it must be emphasised, is purely an illustrative example. It helps to show that there are alternative ways of writing schemas which might describe a music library. Which way the reader would choose in a given circumstance would depend on the following factors:

• the needs of the specification in terms of what exactly has to be encapsulated in it

• consistency, both of style and of content

• the experience of the writer

10.11   Bindings - the theta notation

As the final item in this collection of Z ideas, we discuss briefly the **theta** notation. A **binding** of a schema is one instance of the variables which satisfy the predicate part of the schema in question. When we write the schema name by itself, we are putting forward the whole set of instances which satisfy the predicate. However, when we use the theta notation we are putting forward just one instance. Thus $\theta Members$ would denote a particular instance of the type $Members$ with particular values of the variables declared in $Members$. The theta notation is often used to associate bindings of schemas with values in their current environment. It can be used in making associations between two sets of Δ schemas where it would be tedious to write out all the lines of predicate making the equality between every variable of the two schemas. As an example, we could write a generalised operation on the music library as:

```
┌─MusicLibOperation ─────────────────────────────
│ ΔTwoLibMems      ;           ΔMembers
├─────────────────────────────────────────────────
│ videoMembers'      = videoMembers
│ musicMembers. borrower     = borrower
│ musicMembers. member       = member
│ musicMembers'. borrower    = borrower'
│ musicMembers'. member      = member'
└─────────────────────────────────────────────────
```

This schema could be used to generate more complex operations simply by using the propositional calculus. However, were we to write schemas like the above for much more complex Δ schemas involving many more variables, we would find it somewhat laborious. Instead, we can employ the theta convention and write:

```
┌─MusicLibOperation ─────────────────────────
│ ΔTwoLibMems
│ ΔMembers
├─────────────────────────────────────────────
│ videoMembers'    = videoMembers
│ musicMembers     = θMembers
│ musicMembers'    = θMembers'
└─────────────────────────────────────────────
```

Here all the variables encapsulated in *musicMembers* and *musicMembers'* take on the values current in *Members* and *Members'*.

10.12 Summary

In this chapter we wrote some slightly more complex examples from the music library scenario using the idea of sequences from chapter 8, as well as the ideas of propositional logic and predicate calculus from chapter 6.

We have also introduced some new concepts about the manipulation of Z schemas. These are the ideas of generic definitions, generic schemas, schema normalisation, schema types, bindings and the theta notation.

Exercise

(1) In paragraph 10.4 above the generic definition of *squash* does not use the idea of finite functions, rewrite this definition so that it uses the idea of finite functions introduced in chapter 8.

(2) In the same way that paragraph 10.5 defines a schema to describe the making of a *MemberList,* write a schema which describes the making of an alphabetic list of recordings. Call it *RecordingList.*

(3) Write a generic schema following the example of paragraph 10.7 above to describe the generic analogue of the *ReservEnq* schema of chapter 5 paragraph 5.14.

(4) A schema *NotHeldError* is defined as:

$$NotHeldError \mathrel{\widehat{=}} \neg IsHeld \land$$
$$[report! : Response \mid report! = copyOnLoan\,]$$

By using the following definitions:

$$IsHeld \mathrel{\widehat{=}} [\ held : Copy \nrightarrow Recording\ ;\ copyref? : Copy$$
$$\mid copyref? \in \mathrm{dom}\ held\ ]$$

and $$Response ::= OK \mid alreadyMember \mid copyOnLoan$$

write a correctly normalised schema for $\neg IsHeld$ and comment on anything you find unusual about it.

11

An Introduction to Proofs in Z

11.1 Introduction

Z is a formal language consisting of a set of symbols that can be combined according to its syntactic rules. The preceding chapters have described how we can write legal specifications in this formal language. In this chapter, we investigate what properties of the system can be derived from the schemas with a particular emphasis on the following:

♦ the concept of an axiom

♦ well formed formulae

♦ the semantic turnstile

♦ inference rules

♦ schemas as predicates

♦ making deductions about specifications

11.2 Axioms and well formed formulae

An **axiom** of any formal system is a statement which can be neither proved nor disproved. As such, its validity is taken for granted. An example of an axiomatic formal system is plane geometry. Euclidean plane geometry is an impressive example of how a formal system can be built up from its axiomatic foundation into an elegant structure of interconnected theorems, each of which can be traced indirectly back to the axioms of the system itself.

A **well formulated formula** in any formal language is an expression which has been constructed in accordance with the syntactical rules of the language using symbols drawn from its **alphabet**. An expression constructed according to these two principles is known as a well formulated formula of the formal language and will from now on be referred to as a **wff** (pronounced woof).

Returning to the concept of an axiom, we can consider an axiom to be a wff which can neither be proved nor disproved. The central aim, however, of any formal language is to proceed beyond the axioms of the system and to deduce additional wffs which are theorems of the system. This can only be achieved by the use of an inference system which enables us to prove wffs from the axiomatic basis of the formal language. In the case of **Z**, the inference system is partly based on that of propositional calculus and predicate calculus and the reader is referred to other textbooks for a comprehensive treatment of this area.

11.3 The semantic turnstile

In chapter 6 we introduced the concept of truth tables and considered, in particular, the truth value of the conjunction of two predicates P and Q, written as P $\land$ Q. In that chapter we established that a necessary condition for P $\land$ Q to be **true** is that P is also **true**. Suppose we are now told P $\land$ Q is **true**. As a consequence of this we can deduce that P must also be **true**.

The **semantic turnstile**, $\vdash$, provides a way of recording the above result in the form of a sequent. Whatever premises are 'given' are placed on the left hand side of the turnstile and the deductions that follow as a result of the given premises are placed on the right hand side. In the example above, we can write

$$P \land Q \vdash P \qquad\qquad (11.3.1)$$

We can regard P $\land$ Q as a premise. The conclusion, P, is the theorem that follows logically from the premise after applying the inference rules discussed in the next section.

An axiom, A, which can neither be proved nor disproved can simply be written as:

$$\vdash A$$

indicating that there are no 'given' premises required in order to establish A.

11.4 The propositional calculus inference system

The previous section introduced the concept of a sequent in propositional calculus which places the premises on the left hand side of the semantic turnstile and the deduction on the right hand side. The steps required to proceed from the premises to the deduction constitute the 'proof'. Each step in the proof has to be justified by utilising the inference rules of propositional calculus, some of which are now summarised. A full and exhaustive treatment of this area is beyond the scope of this text.

11.4.1 Modus ponens

The rule of modus ponendo ponens (usually abbreviated to **modus ponens**) states that if we are given as premises P and P $\Rightarrow$ Q, we can deduce Q. In other words, Q can be deduced on the assumption that both P and P $\Rightarrow$ Q are also **true**. This rule forms one of the cornerstones of propositional calculus. It can be summarised as a sequent in the following form:

$$P,\ P \Rightarrow Q \vdash Q \qquad\qquad (11.4.1)$$

in which we note that the premises on the LHS are separated by commas.

Example 1
Consider the statement:

if the computer is an IBM compatible PC, then the operating system is DOS

This statement can be captured by implication and expressed in the form:

$$P \Rightarrow Q$$

where P denotes the proposition 'the computer is an IBM compatible PC' and Q the proposition 'the operating system is DOS'. If we are now given as a premise, P, that the computer under consideration is in actual fact a PC, we expect to correctly conclude that the operating system is DOS.

11.4.2 Modus tonens

Modus tollendo tonens (usually abbreviated to **modus tollens**) is another inference rule of propositional calculus. This can be written as a sequent in the form:

$$\neg Q,\ P \Rightarrow Q \vdash \neg P$$

Example 2
We again consider the statement

if the computer is an IBM compatible PC, then the operating system is DOS

which as we have seen in the modus ponens example can be written as

$P \Rightarrow Q$

with P denoting the proposition 'the computer is a PC' and Q denoting 'the operating system is DOS'. In the case of modus tollens, we are given that the operating system is not DOS, which is represented symbolically by $\neg Q$, and we conclude that the computer is not an IBM compatible PC.

11.4.3 And elimination (∧ elimination)

The rule of and-elimination is another rule which is of fundamental importance in propositional calculus. It is actually summarised as a sequent in (11.3.1) and states that if we are given a conjunction which is **true**, then each of the conjuncts must separately be **true**. Using this rule we can arrive at two separate and equally valid conclusions:

$P \wedge Q \vdash P$ (∧ elimination)

or

$P \wedge Q \vdash Q$ (∧ elimination)

Example 3
In this elementary example we show how a proof in propositional calculus is presented. Consider the compound statement:

the number 2 is prime and also even

We will let P denote the premise the number 2 is prime and Q that it is even. The conjunction of these two premises is $P \wedge Q$. From this conjunction, we wish to prove that 2 is an even number.

Each step in a proof using propositional calculus is justified by appealing to the inference rules. Moreover, each step is presented on a separate line which is numbered sequentially. The starting point in any proof using propositional calculus is with one of the given premises and the proof is sometimes referred to as a **derivation**.

The proof in this case proceeds as follows:

1   (1) $P \wedge Q$ (assumption)
1   (2) Q   (1, ∧ elimination)

In this example we note that the first number on the left refers to the single premise which is given as an assumption. Since each line depends on this single premise it also appears on the second line of the proof. The remaining bracketed number on the left is a line number which is incremented by 1 as each line of the proof proceeds. On the right hand side of each line the particular inference rule used to justify each step is cited, preceded by the number of the line to which the rule is applied.

11.4.4 Disjunction elimination (∨ elimination)

The rule of disjunction elimination states that if we have a conclusion, C, which can be derived separately from each disjunct of a given disjunction A ∨ B, we can deduce C. This is one of the more complicated rules of the propositional calculus inference system and it can be summarised most clearly in the form of three separate sequents:

(1) A ⊢ C

(2) B ⊢ C

(3) A ∨ B ⊢ C

The first theorem states that C can be derived from A(line 1) and the second that C can be derived from B(line 2). The conclusion, which is arrived at by ∨ elimination, is that C can be derived on the assumption that A ∨ B is true. The vital step to observe in this line of reasoning is that if the disjunction A ∨ B is true then at least one of the disjuncts is true or both are true.

An example of ∨ elimination
As an illustration of the use of disjunction elimination, suppose we are asked to prove the sequent P ∨ Q, P ⇒ M, Q ⇒ M ⊢ M. The derivation proceeds as follows:

1	(1) P ∨ Q	(assumption)
1	(2) P	(assumption)
2	(3) P ⇒ M	(assumption)
1, 2	(4) M	(2, 3 modus ponens)
1	(5) Q	(assumption)
3	(6) Q ⇒ M	(assumption)
1, 3	(7) M	(5, 6 modus ponens)
1,2,3	(8) M	(∨ elimination)

11.4.5 Or introduction

This rule states that if we are given a proposition, we can form a disjunction of it with any other proposition. Suppose, for example, we are given P as an assumption. The rule of ∨ introduction states that we can now introduce another proposition Q and form the disjunction P ∨ Q.

11.4.6 And introduction

The rule of ∧ introduction states that if a proposition, P, is true and we have another proposition, Q, which is also true then we can form the conjunction P ∧ Q.

This rule can be written in the form of a sequent as:

P, Q ⊢ P ∧ Q   (∧ introduction)

11.5 Predicate calculus inference rules

The previous sections have considered some of the rules of the propositional calculus inference system. These rules apply specifically to propositions and our motivation in studying them is that they can be more generally applied to predicates which, as we have seen in chapter 6, we can regard as propositions with a variable. Since **Z** schemas generally involve predicates rather than propositions, it is time for us to consider some of the rules of the predicate calculus inference system.

11.5.1 Universal elimination

Consider the predicate $\forall x : T \bullet P(x)$. This will be true for all values of x drawn or selected from the type T. Let us select an arbitrary value, a, from the type T. For this particular value, a, since it is selected from a set which is universally quantified, we can state that a has the property, $P(a)$. This is known as the rule of universal elimination and can be summarised as follows:

$\forall x : T \mid a \in T, P(x) \bullet P(a)$

where a is either arbitrarily selected from T or is a specific value.

11.5.2 Universal introduction

To eliminate the universal quantifier by assigning a specific value to the variable quantified is an easy step. The reverse process is much more difficult. To introduce a universal quantifier, we must be sure that the variable concerned can be selected quite arbitrarily from the domain of interest. Universal introduction can be stated as follows:

$a \in T, P(a) \vdash \forall x : T \bullet P(x)$

provided a can be selected arbitrarily from the set T.

11.5.3 Existential elimination

The previous two subsections introduced the rules for the universal quantifier. In the case of the existential quantifier, similar rules apply.

Consider the statement $\exists x : T \bullet P(x)$. This asserts that there is at least one value of x belonging to type T such that $P(x)$ is true. A particular value of x that satisfies the rule $\exists x : T \bullet P(x)$ we will quite arbitrarily decide to call a. Any suitable name, however, can be used as a replacement for the quantified variable. Hence, we can state the rule of existential elimination as:

$$\exists x : T, P(x) \vdash a \in T \bullet P(a)$$

where a is a specific value.

11.5.4 Existential introduction

The existential quantifier can be introduced if we know that a predicate is true for a certain value. Suppose, for example, we know that $P(x)$ is **true** when x has the value a i.e. $P(a)$ is true. This enables us to assert that there is at least one value of x that satisfies $P(x)$. This can be written as:

$$a \in T, P(a) \vdash \exists x : T \bullet P(x)$$

This rule enables us to introduce the existential quantifier when it is known that a predicate is **true** for a specific value.

11.6 Schemas as predicates

We begin this section with an example. Consider the theorem:

$$\exists x : \mathbb{Z} \mid x > 0 \wedge x \bmod 2 = 0 \vdash x^2 = 4 \qquad (11.6.1)$$

which states that there is a number, x, greater than zero and belonging to the set $\mathbb{Z}$, which is also an even number. In this example, everything to the left of the semantic turnstile can be placed into a **Z** schema which, appropriately, we will call *TwoSquared*.

```
┌─TwoSquared ────────
│   x : ℤ
├────────────────────
│   x > 0
│
│   x mod 2 = 0
└────────────────────
```

The introduction of this **Z** schema enables us to rewrite (11.6.1) more succinctly in the form:

$$\exists TwoSquared \vdash x^2 = 4 \qquad\qquad (11.6.2)$$

in which the existential quantifier is applied to the declaration part of the schema *TwoSquared*. The conclusion, $x^2 = 4$, can also be captured in a **Z** schema, *Result*, as follows:

```
┌─ Result ────────

   x : ℤ
  ─────────────────
   x² = 4
└─────────────────
```

The theorem (11.6.1) can now be rewritten as

$$\exists TwoSquared \vdash Result \qquad\qquad (11.6.3)$$

This example shows that Z schemas can be used on both the left and right hand side of theorems. It is only the predicate part of a schema on the right hand side that is used so, in effect, the declaration part of that schema is not required. It is perfectly safe to discard the declarations of the schema to the right of the semantic turnstile, provided they are captured in the declaration part of the schema on the left hand side.

11.7 Formal reasoning applied to the initial state

The previous sections in this chapter have presented some of the inference rules of propositional logic and predicate calculus. We have also seen that a **Z** schema is a convenient way of writing predicates, so it is now appropriate for us to consider the application of these inference rules, in order that we can make deductions about schemas.

In chapter 1 we introduced the following state invariant schema for a bookshop:

```
┌─BookShop ────────

   storage : Book ↔ Place

   stock : Book ↔ ℕ₁
  ─────────────────
   dom storage = dom stock
└─────────────────
```

The state invariant schema captures all the valid states of a system both before and after any operations on the system. In particular, the predicates in the state invariant schema represent fundamental relationships that must always hold, irrespective of the operation and hence are invariant.

We now wish to consider the initial state of this bookshop which is given by the schema, *InitBookShop*:

```
┌─InitBookShop ──────────
│
│   BookShop'
│  ─────────────
│   storage' = Ø
│
│   stock' = Ø
└──────────────────
```

The initial state theorem asserts that given the state invariant schema of a system there is a special value of this corresponding to the initial requirements. We would like to prove that the schema, *InitBookShop*, satisfies the initial state of the bookshop and also satisfies the state invariant schema. The initial state theorem can be summarised as follows:

⊢ ∃ *BookShop'* • *InitBookShop*

The schema, *InitBookShop*, corresponds to the initial state of the bookshop when it has no books in stock. Replacing *BookShop'* by its expansion in terms of predicates we have:

⊢ ∃ *storage'* : *Book* ↔ *Place*; *stock'* : *Book* ↔ $\mathbb{N}_1$ |
   dom *stock'* = dom *storage'* •
   storage' = Ø ∧ *stock'* = Ø

We note from this that the requirement that dom *stock'* = dom *storage'* is satisfied when both *storage'* and *stock'* are empty sets. Since the filtering predicate must be satisfied, we can remove the constraint bar and introduce another conjunction.

⊢ ∃ *storage'* : *Book* ↔ *Place*; *stock'* : *Book* ↔ $\mathbb{N}_1$ •
   dom *stock'* = dom *storage'* ∧
   storage' = Ø ∧ *stock'* = Ø

In this example the existential quantification is over *storage'* and *stock'* and the last two conjunctions introduce an explicit value for these relationships, namely the empty set Ø. The existential quantifier rule given earlier states that the quantification can be removed if an exact value for the quantified variable is given and all occurrences of the quantified variable are replaced by that value. Dropping the existential quantifier and making the appropriate substitutions gives:

$$\vdash \varnothing \in Book \leftrightarrow Place \wedge \varnothing \in Book \leftrightarrow \mathbb{N}_1 \wedge \text{dom } \varnothing = \text{dom } \varnothing$$

We now need to prove each of the following conjuncts separately.

$$\varnothing \in Book \leftrightarrow Place \tag{11.7.1}$$

$$\varnothing \in Book \leftrightarrow \mathbb{N}_1 \tag{11.7.2}$$

$$\text{dom } \varnothing = \text{dom } \varnothing \tag{11.7.3}$$

Firstly, we note that (11.7.3) is an identity and therefore **true**. With regard to (11.7.1), we note that $Book \leftrightarrow Place : \mathbb{P}(Book \times Place)$ and $\varnothing \in \mathbb{P}(Book \times Place)$. Similar arguments apply to the second conjunct, $\varnothing \in Book \leftrightarrow \mathbb{N}_1$ from which it follows that both (11.7.1) and (11.7.2) are **true**. Since the conjunction of all 3 conjuncts is therefore **true**, we conclude that *InitBookShop* satisfies the initial state of the bookshop.

11.8 Summary

In this chapter we have attempted to outline the application of formal reasoning to Z schemas. We have applied formal reasoning in one particular area, known as the initial state theorem. However, in practice, such techniques are capable of much wider application to deriving additional properties of the system under investigation.

Exercise
(1) Prove that the initial state schema of the music library given in chapter 5 section 10 page 84, satisfies the music library state invariant schema (chapter 5 section 7 page 81).

12

Z-Developments and Variations

12.1 Introduction

The purpose of this chapter is to review the current state of **Z** as a formal method and to summarise the recent developments and diversifications which have taken place.

The general term software crisis is used to refer to the potentially intractable problems associated with software development. Activities such as analysis, design and programming take much longer than expected and cause projects to overrun completion dates with the further consequence that development costs are much higher than originally estimated. Over the last decade, in an attempt to find solutions to the software crisis, more and more software development has involved formal methods and **Z** is one of the most widely used. However, the majority of the uses of formal methods has taken place in the academic community rather than in the industrial environment. Even though industrial experience has been limited to date, formal methods have been shown to be effective in the development of large scale projects including safety critical applications. The need for a rigorous approach to software specification has recently been recognised by the UK Ministry of Defence who, in their interim defence standard 00-55 [1], has mandated that all safety critical software should be specified and developed using a formal method.

Communication systems have also been popular areas for the application of formal methods as they exhibit challenging technical features such as concurrency and distribution. Open systems interconnection requires interfaces and services to be specified precisely. The ISO began work in 1980 on standardising the specification of communication systems, for example with ESTELLE (Extended finite state machine language, ISO 9074) and LOTUS (Language of Temporal Ordering Specification, ISO 8807) for formal specification of open system standards.

Research into the use of formal methods for software development has been concentrated on safety critical and highly complex systems. However, following the reports of the successful use of **Z** to assist in the re-development of the CICS system at the IBM-UK Laboratories in 1987 (Wordsworth, 1987 [2], Johnson, 1987 [3]) a number of workers in very different fields investigated the application of **Z** and other formal methods. Rees, 1992 [4] has described the use of **Z** in the development of computerised information systems for the Trans Manche Super Train for the Channel Tunnel. The system requires a number of programmable logic controllers and real time computers distributed along its length. **Z** was used both to write parts of the specification and to verify parts of the specification written in English. Recent research has indicated that formal methods can have much wider applications than merely being confined to safety critical systems. In a further development, French *et al.*,1992 [5] have investigated the usefulness of formal methods, particularly VDM, in the sphere of operational research.

As formal methods have been extended into new application areas, a number of developments have been suggested. One such recent divergence or development from basic **Z** has been to embed **Z** notation into structured systems methodologies. The objective of combining requirements capture and structuring techniques with formal methods is to facilitate mathematical proof such as would be required for verification of safety critical systems. By a structured methodology we mean an approach to software development which breaks a system down into component parts so that data and processes can be treated separately. Such methods have the advantage that while they impose a discipline on software development, the diagrams produced can be understood intuitively by the non-expert user. One area for future developments is this linkage between the semi-formal and the formal techniques. Bradley (1988) [6] reported the results of applying the combined method to a number of specifications in the avionics sphere and Clarke (1988) [7] also described how formal methods can be incorporated into the software development life-cycle. Semmens and Allen, (1990) [8] have described a method which combines Yourdon's structured design method and **Z**, while Polack, Whiston and Hitchcock [9] have reported the development of a method for writing **Z** specifications using SSADM version 4.

12.2 Objected oriented Z

Another approach is based upon the development of a link between **Z** and object oriented methods. The key factor that distinguishes object oriented approaches from other structured systems methodologies is that the method is based on objects and classes [10]. An object is a physical object, person or some abstract idea and a class is a common description of a collection of objects. An object is usually described by a collection of data called attributes. Each class has a collection of operations which can change or read this associated data.

Object oriented methods also introduce two powerful concepts i.e.

♦ inheritance as a means of creating new classes by modifying definitions of existing classes, so that, for example the objects belonging to one class are a special case of the objects of another class

♦ composition, where objects of one class are built in some way from the objects of another class

It is claimed [11] that object oriented methods lead to specifications which are shorter and simpler to comprehend and to structure, and that therefore this gives a greater understanding of the system being specified.

A number of workers have suggested extensions to **Z** to incorporate object oriented concepts [12]. Rose *et al.* [13] have proposed Object **Z** and Cusack [14] and Rafsanjani [15] have proposed ZEST following Cusack's work on 'Inheritance in Object Oriented **Z**'.

One of the problems of marrying object oriented methods to **Z** is that, in contradiction to the concept of inheritance, **Z** treats types as disjoint sets so that no basic type can be a subset of another type in the same specification. There are a number of variations of object oriented methods. Some object oriented methods would create great difficulty for integration with **Z**. For example, Martin and Odell's [11] approach allows an object to change its class, a concept which would make type declaration in **Z** very difficult. Both Object **Z** and ZEST seek to resolve some of these problems by specifying each class as though it were a separate **Z** specification.

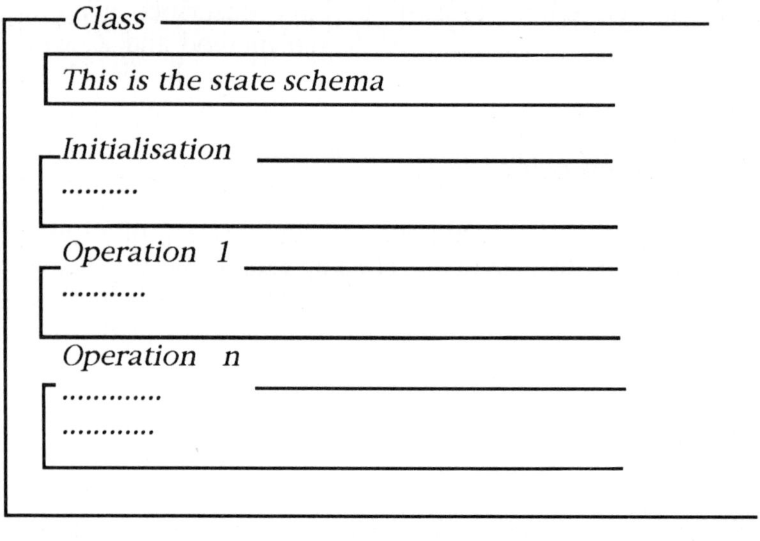

Fig. 12.1 Class schema in object oriented Z

Each class has a set of states specified by a state schema, an initialisation schema and a set of operations which act on the state, each operation being specified by an operation schema. All schemas associated with a particular class are collected together in a single box called the class schema as illustrated in Fig. 12.1 above.

Another area of difficulty with object oriented extensions to **Z** is the use of message passing in object oriented design. This is based on the concept of one object sending a request to another object for a particular operation to be performed. Message passing is allowed between objects and classes. ZEST does not provide for message passing at present.

Several researchers are working in this direction including Giovanni and Iachini, (1990) [16], who attempted to integrate **Z** with HOOD the object oriented design methodology which is the standard European Space Agency design method. The HOOD methodology was capable of delivering improvements in cost and productivity but not necessarily in terms of quality and reliability. The approach taken by Giovanni and Iachini was to formally describe the HOOD objects and rigorously verify some properties in **Z**. In another case, Swatman and Swatman, (1992) [17] have worked with industrial partners in the USA to investigate the application of formal specifications in **Z** and Object **Z** within the domain of Management Information Systems. In the UK, Wilson (1992) [18] has reported work on object oriented analysis and formal methods in an industrial application at BT. Wilson was looking for an approach which would combine the precision of mathematics, the simplicity and clarity of diagrams similar to those found in traditional structured analysis and the flexibility and reusability offered by object orientation. He therefore adopted Yourdon's [10] approach to provide a basic structure and to use an object oriented extension of **Z** to provide the detail. In this way the object oriented diagrams provided the primary specification but where greater precision were needed the power of **Z** was available.

There are, however, fears that some of these developments could lead to a divergence in the original **Z** method. The ZIP project (Hepworth, (1990) [19]) is an attempt at unification which is intended to align and standardise the development of **Z** methods and tools in keeping with the standard notation based on the **Z** reference manual.

12.3 Automated tools

No one is claiming however that formal methods will provide an instant, cheap and perfect solution to all the problems of software development. One of the main criticism of **Z** is that it takes time and effort to go through the long learning curve to develop skills in using the method. This also tends to mean that coding a project does not start until relatively later in the project than would be the case in other methods. This is not actually a disadvantage as the quality of the code should therefore be higher and take less time to produce, test and debug.

One of the main problems with the use of formal methods is the lack of tools. Although **Z** editors, type and syntax checkers are available there is a great need for cross-references and proof tools [20]. At the moment it is still the case that most formal specifications are prepared laboriously with pencil and paper.

The provision of automated tools such as type checkers and syntax checkers is essential to the successful application of **Z** to industrial scale problems. The advantages that automated tools would bring include the reduction of the possibility of errors, improved software quality and increased productivity. In the case of safety critical systems formal methods have been shown to reduce the likelihood of serious failures and, therefore, the ability to provide large scale development through the use of automated tools would be a key advantage.

Although **Z** notation has been shown to be effective in a number of industrial projects, one of the disadvantages that has resulted from these pioneering specifications is that a number of different **Z** tools have evolved. Some of these tools which have become available for specification development in **Z** have been reported by Parker in "Z Tools Catalogue", (1991) [21].

Recently researchers at the University of York [22] have developed the CADiZ system, an integrated computer aided design tool in **Z**, which has been developed to check and type set **Z** specifications. Vasconcelos and McDermid [23] have reported the development of a hypertext style integrated tool and user interface as an extension to CADiZ.

Jones (1992) [24] has reported on the development of a prototype ICL **Z** proof support tool which has been used to specify and verify the critical properties of secure systems. A further development in the area of software tools has been centred around attempts to animate **Z** specifications [25]. For example, West and Eaglestone (1992) [26] advocate the use of a system whereby the **Z** specification may be animated as Prolog programs. These researchers have used two **Z**/Prolog translation strategies - formal program synthesis and structure simulation. The second method was developed for implementing several case studies.

12.4 Summary

There are many advantages to the use of formal methods for software specification. These include:

♦ the use of a high level abstract language encourages clear logical design

♦ it is possible to verify formally that the implementation meets the requirements specification

♦ software development should be more reliable and maintenance can be carried out in an ordered manner, since the effect that any change will have on the rest of the system can be reasoned about

References

1. MoD 'Interim Defence Standard 00-55', Issue 1, April 1991.

2. Wordsworth , J.B. (1987) Formal Methods in the development of CICS. *Computer Bulletin.* 3 pt.4. pp6-7.

3. Johnson, P. (1987) Using Z with CICS. *Proc. SEAS Anniversary Meeting* . 1. pp 303-34.

4. Rees, C. (1992) Experiences of using formal methods within the TMST project. *GEC Journal of Research,* Vol 10, No1.

5. French, A.P. , McKeown, G.P., Rayward-Smith,V.J. (1992) Experiences of using formal specification techniques for operation research problems. *Proc. Unified Computation Laboratory.* (Eds. Rattray, C., Clarke, R.G., pp233-42, Oxford Univ Press.

6. Bradley, A. (1988) Embedding formal methods in SAFRA. *Proc. Software engineering and its applications to avionics,* pp 10/1-9, AGARD.

7. Clarke, S. (1988) The increasing importance of formal methods (software engineering). *Computer Bulletin.* 4 pt.1 pp22-3.

8. Semmens, L. and Allen,P. (1990)Using Yourdon and Z: an approach to formal specification . *Z User Workshop* (Eds. Nicholls, J.E. *et al.*) Oxford, Springer-Verlag.

9. Polack, F., Whiston, M. and Hitchcock, P. (1990) Structured Analysis - draft method for writing Z specifications. *Z User Workshop.*

10. Coad, P. and Yourdon, E. (1991). *Object oriented analysis.* Prentice Hall .

11. Martin, J., Odell, J.J. (1992) *Object oriented analysis and design..* Prentice Hall.

12. Holt, R., deChampeaux, D. (1992) A framework for using formal methods in object oriented software development. *OOPS Messenger.* 3 No. 2, pp9-10.

13. Duke, D., King, P., Rose. G.A. and Smith, G. (1991). Object -**Z** specification language, version 1. *Technical Report 91-1, Software   Verification Research Centre.* Dept. of Computer Science, University of Queensland.

14. Cusack, E. (1991). Inheritance in object oriented **Z**. *ECOOP '91, European Conference on object oriented programming* (Ed. America, P.) pp. 167-179, Springer-Verlag.

15. Rafsanjani, G.H. (1993) ZEST: **Z** extended with structuring ' *Internal BT report .*

16. Giovanni, R. and Iachini, P. (1990) HOOD and **Z** for the development of complex systems. *VDM'90. VDM and Z Formal methods in software development .* (Eds. Bjorner et al.)pp. 262-289. Springer-Verlag.

17 Swatman , P.A. and Swatman, P.M.C. (1992) *Proc. International Conference on Organisation and Information Systems.* (Eds. Kaltnekar, **Z**).

18. Wilson, J.C.R. (1993) Formal methods in object oriented analysis. *BT Technology Journal,* 11,3, pp18-31.

19. Hepworth , B. (1990) ZIP - a unification initiative for **Z** standards, methods & tools. *Z User Workshop. Proc. of fourth annual Z user meeting,* pp 253-9. Springer-Verlag.

20. Sennet, C. (1987) Review of type checking and scope rules of specification language **Z**. *Report No. 87017, Royal Signals and Radar establishment,* Malvern , U.K.

21. Parker, C.E. (1991) **Z** Tools Catalogue , *ZIP Project Technical Report* **Z**IP/BAe/90/020.

22. The CADi**Z** Tutorial. (1991). *York Software Engineering Limited.* YSE, University of York.

23. Vasconcelos, M.L. and McDermid, J.A. (1993) Incremental processing of **Z** specifications. *IFIP Transactions (Communication Systems)* C-10, pp53-69.

24. Jones, R.B. (1992) Methods and tools for the specification of critical propertise. *Proc. 5th Refinement Workshop* (Eds. Jones. C.B., Shaw R.C., Denvir, T.) pp88-118. Springer-Verlag.

25. Knott, R., Krause, P. and Cozens, J. (1990). Computer aided transformations of **Z** into Prolog. *Z User Workshop* (Eds. Nicholls, J.E. *et al.*) Oxford, Springer-Verlag.

26. West, M. and Eaglestone, B. (1992) Software development: two approaches to animation of **Z** specifications using Prolog. Software Engineering Journal.

Appendix A

A music library specification

A.1 Introduction

In this appendix we collect together some of the previously written schemas and definitions from the main chapters in this book and put them together with others into a coherent specification for the music library. In particular, the appendix gives an illustration of a style which may be used when writing **Z** specifications, by showing how natural language text can be interspersed with mathematical statements.

A.2 Given sets (basic types)

Our music library is concerned with a number of members who may borrow copies of recordings held by the library. Members may also may make reservations for particular recordings, if they find that all the copies of the recordings they would like to borrow are already on loan to other members.

We thus declare the basic types to be used in the remainder of the specification as:

$$[\, Person, Recording, Copy \,]$$

Person is the set of all unique people, some of whom may at some stage become members of the library. *Recording* is the set of all unique recordings. We do not need to elaborate on this further; we need not concern ourselves with unnecessary detail such as what precisely makes one recording different from another. *Copy* is the set of identifiers from which the library chooses particular values to distinguish all the different copies of the various recordings which they hold.

A.3 The state invariant

We now proceed to write the state invariant of the music library. It should be stated that this state invariant represents just one possible state invariant that could be written about the music library. It is concerned with defining those objects in the library system that we are initially interested in. Other versions of the state invariant could be written to define other objects of differing interest.

```
┌─MusicLib ──────────────────────────
│  member              : ℙ Person
│  held                : Copy ↠ Recording
│  loan                : Copy ↠ Person
│  reservation         : Recording ↔ Person
├─────────────────────────────────────
│  dom loan            ⊆ dom held
│  ran loan            ⊆ member
│  dom reservation     ⊆ ran held
│  ran reservation     ⊆ member
└─────────────────────────────────────
```

The explanation of the mathematical statements can be found in section 5.8 in chapter 5. In natural language we would say that we have defined:

• a set of members (*member*) as a subset of all people
• a set of holdings (*held*) of a number of copies, some of which may be of the same recording
• a set of loans (*loan*), where some copies are loaned out to some people; with the possibility that someone could borrow more than one copy, but a copy cannot be on loan to more than one person
• a set of reservations (*reservation*), whereby some recordings are reserved by some people

The predicate part of the state invariant states that:

• the copies out on loan are actually held by the library
• the people taking out loans are actually members of the library
• the reservations being made are for recordings held by the library
• the people making the reservations are actually members of the library

A.4 The initial state

Before describing any actions on the library it is usual to describe the library's initial state before any members join and before any recordings are added to the collection. This is done with the initial state schema:

```
┌─Init ─────────────
│  MusicLib'
├────────────────────
│  member' = Ø
│  held'   = Ø
└────────────────────
```

This states that after a library is brought into being, it starts with no members and no recordings in its collection. These two conditions also make sure that initially no loans or reservations exist either.

A.5 Adding a new member

We next describe the operation of adding a new member to the membership list of the library:

```
┌─AddNewMem ─────────────────────
│ ΔMusicLib
│ mem?   :Person
├────────────────────────────────
│ mem?  ∉ member
│ member' = member ∪ {mem?}
│ held'    = held
│ loan'    = loan
│ reservation' = reservation
└────────────────────────────────
```

This schema defines a new member (*mem?*) and states that this new member is not already a member of the library. It then goes on to state that the new membership list is made up of the old membership list with the addition of the new member.

However, there needs also to be a protection against the error condition that the *mem?* is already a member. We do this by, firstly, defining an enumerated type, which describes messages the system might provide in various circumstances:

Response ::= *OK* | *alreadyMember* | *alreadyHeld* | *errorOnRemoval* | *reservedPutOnSide* | *errorOnLoan* | *errorOnReserve*

As well as being used for this particular error condition the type, *Response*, also enumerates responses to other conditions we encounter later on in the specification.

We then write a schema to describe the error condition of trying to add a member who already is a member:

```
┌─AddNewMemError ─────────
│ ΞMusicLib
│ mem?  : Person
│ reply! : Response
├─────────────────────────
│ mem?  ∈ member
│ reply! = alreadyMember
└─────────────────────────
```

This describes the case where an output is given stating that the person is already a member. Additionally, by means of the ΞMusicLib statement, it states that the membership list remains unchanged.

To complete the description of error conditions we need a further small schema to describe the output message for a non error condition:

$$OKMessage \cong [reply! : Response \mid reply! = OK]$$

Now we can write a new schema *EnrolNewMem* which encompasses both the case where the member being presented for admission is already a member and when s/he is not:

$$EnrolNewMem \cong (AddNewMem \wedge OKMessage) \vee \\ AddNewMemError$$

A.6 Adding a new copy

We next write schemas to describe the addition of a copy of a recording to the library. The first schema describes the non error condition:

```
┌─AddCopy ──────────────────────────
│ ΔMusicLib
│ copyref?          : Copy
│ record?           : Recording
├───────────────────────────────────
│ copyref?          ∉ dom held
│ held'    = held ∪ {copyref? ↦ record?}
│ member'           = member
│ loan'             = loan
│ reservation'      = reservation
└───────────────────────────────────
```

This describes the case where we have the new copy (*copyref?*) of the recording (*record?*) and again there is a condition that the *copyref?* is not already held by the library.

Once more we need to allow for the possibility that the *copyref?* is already in the library's collection by means of a similar technique as when we found that the input, *mem?*, could already be a member. We thus write a schema to describe the error condition of trying to add a copy which is already held by the library:

```
┌─AddCopyError ──────────────
│  ΞMusicLib
│  copyref?              : Copy
│  record?               : Recording
│  reply!                : Response
├─────────────────────────────
│  copyref?              ∈ dom held
│  reply!                = alreadyHeld
└─────────────────────────────
```

This describes the case where an output is given stating that the copy is already held. Additionally, by means of the ΞMusicLib statement, it states that the collection remains unchanged.

Now we write a new schema *AddNewCopy* which encompasses both the case where the copy being presented for addition is already in the collection and when it is not:

$$AddNewCopy \cong (AddCopy \land OKMessage) \lor$$
$$AddCopyError$$

We note in passing that we have no need to write schemas to add new recordings to the library. This automatically occurs when we add new copies to the system. If the new copy is of a new recording, then the description of that recording will be added in the maplet:
copyref? ↦ *record?*. There is no provision in this current view of the system for details of recordings to be held by the system without there being any copies of them. Similarly, copies cannot be added to the system without being of a particular recording.

A.7 Removing a member

We write the schemas for the operation of removing a member using exactly the same reasoning as when we wrote those for adding a member, except that, in this case, an error condition occurs when the member being requested for deletion is not a member of the library. Additionally, we propose that it would be an error for a member to be removed from the lists, both if s/he had recordings out on loan, and if s/he had made reservations for any recordings.

Thus the normal non error schema is:

```
┌─RemoveMem ──────────────
│ ΔMusicLib
│ mem?   :Person
├──────────────────────────
│ mem?   ∈ member
│ mem?   ∉ ran loan
│ mem?   ∉ ran reservation
│ member' = member \ {mem?}
│ held'   = held
│ loan'   = loan
│ reservation' = reservation
└──────────────────────────
```

We go on to write the schema for the error condition where we try to remove a member but cannot, for one of the three reasons: a) that s/he is not a member, b) that s/he has an outstanding loan or c) that s/he has an outstanding reservation:

```
┌─RemoveMemError ──────────
│ ΞMusicLib
│ mem?  : Person
│ reply! : Response
├──────────────────────────
│ (mem?  ∉ member      ∨
│  mem?  ∈ ran loan    ∨
│  mem?  ∈ ran reservation)
│  reply! = errorOnRemoval
└──────────────────────────
```

We can thus write the schema for describing both cases; where there is no error condition, and the case where there is:

$$RemoveExistMem \;\hat{=}\; (RemoveMem \wedge OKMessage) \vee$$
$$RemoveMemError$$

A.8 Removing a copy

In a similar manner to the above procedure for removing members from membership lists we can remove copies from the lists. Here, we always have to remove a maplet of the form *copyref?* ↦ *record?* from the list of copies held. First the non error case:

```
┌─RemoveCopy ──────────────────────────────────────
│ ΔMusicLib
│ copyref?              : Copy
│ record?               : Recording
├───────────────────────────────────────────────────
│ {copyref? ↦ record?}  ∈ held
│ copyref?              ∉ dom loan
│ record? ∈ dom reservation ⇒ ¬(∃₁ c : Copy • c ↦ record? ∈ held)
│ held'                 = held \ {copyref? ↦ record?}
│ member'               = member
│ loan'                 = loan
│ reservation'          = reservation
└───────────────────────────────────────────────────
```

This has three preconditions for non error operation:

• that the copy of the recording in question is actually held by the library
• that the copy is not out on loan
• that if this recording is reserved by someone then there is more than one copy held in the library.

Moving on to the error schema we can write:

```
┌─RemoveCopyError ─────────────────────────────────
│ ΞMusicLib
│ copyref?              : Copy
│ record?               : Recording
│ reply!                : Response
├───────────────────────────────────────────────────
│ ({copyref? ↦ record?}          ∉ held     ∨
│ copyref?              ∈ dom loan           ∨
│ ((∃₁ c : Copy • c ↦ record? ∈ held) ∧ record? ∈ dom reservation ))
│ reply!                = errorOnRemoval
└───────────────────────────────────────────────────
```

This will describe error conditions which occur, either when the copy of that recording is not held by the library, or when that copy is out on loan, or when there is only one copy of the recording in question and there is an outstanding reservation for it.

Lastly in this section we can write the complete schema for copy removal:

$$RemoveExistCopy \triangleq (RemoveCopy \wedge OKMessage) \vee$$
$$RemoveCopyError$$

A.9 Making a loan

Moving on to the basic functions of a library, we write a schema which describes the loan of a recording to a member:

```
┌─MakeLoan ─────────────────────────────────────
│ ΔMusicLib
│ mem?              : Person
│ copyref?          : Copy
├───────────────────────────────────────────────
│ mem?              ∈ member
│ copyref?          ∈ dom held
│ copyref?          ∉ dom loan
│ held copyref? ∈ dom reservation ⇒
│                   mem? ∈ reservation (｜{ held copyref? }｜)
│ loan'             = loan ∪ {copyref? ↦ mem?}
│ member'           = member
│ held'             = held
│ reservation'      = reservation \ {held copyref? ↦ mem?}
└───────────────────────────────────────────────
```

This incorporates three preconditions: a) that the member is a member of the library, b) that the copy is both held by the library and not already out on loan, and c) that if the recording of which the copy is about to be loaned is already reserved, then the member making the loan must be one of the members having reserved the recording.

We can thus write the error schema as:

```
┌─MakeLoanError ────────────────────────────────
│ ΞMusicLib
│ mem?              : Person
│ copyref?          : Copy
│ reply!            : Response
├───────────────────────────────────────────────
│ (mem?             ∉ member          ∨
│ copyref?          ∉ dom held        ∨
│ copyref?          ∈ dom loan        ∨
│ (held copyref? ∈ dom reservation    ∧
│                   mem? ∉ reservation (｜{ held copyref? }｜)))
│ reply!            = errorOnLoan
└───────────────────────────────────────────────
```

The full schema for making loans would be:

$$MakeProperLoan \cong (MakeLoan \wedge OKMessage) \vee MakeLoanError$$

A.10 Returning a loan

The next schema describes the operation of returning a copy of a recording:

$$
\begin{array}{l}
\rule{8cm}{0.4pt}\\
ReturnLoan \\
\Delta MusicLib \\
mem? \qquad\qquad : Person \\
copyref? \qquad\quad : Copy \\
reply! \qquad\qquad : Response \\
\rule{8cm}{0.4pt}\\
mem? \qquad\qquad \in member \\
copyref? \qquad\quad \in \mathrm{dom}\ held \\
copyref? \qquad\quad \in \mathrm{dom}\ loan \\
held\ copyref? \in \mathrm{dom}\ reservation \Rightarrow reply! = reservedPutOnSide \\
loan' \qquad\qquad\ \ = loan \setminus \{copyref? \mapsto mem?\} \\
member' \qquad\quad = member \\
held' \qquad\qquad\ \ = held \\
reservation' \qquad = reservation \\
\rule{8cm}{0.4pt}
\end{array}
$$

This schema has two preconditions:

• that the member returning the copy is a member of the library
• that the copy being returned is both held by the library and out on loan

Additionally it provides an output message if the recording has been reserved by another member.

We proceed by writing the error schema as:

$$
\begin{array}{l}
\rule{8cm}{0.4pt}\\
ReturnLoanError \\
\Xi MusicLib \\
mem? \qquad\qquad : Person \\
copyref? \qquad\quad : Copy \\
reply! \qquad\qquad : Response \\
\rule{8cm}{0.4pt}\\
(mem? \qquad\qquad \notin member \qquad\quad \lor \\
copyref? \qquad\quad \notin \mathrm{dom}\ held \qquad \lor \\
copyref? \qquad\quad \notin \mathrm{dom}\ loan) \\
reply! \qquad\qquad = errorOnLoan \\
\rule{8cm}{0.4pt}
\end{array}
$$

Thus the full schema for returning loans would be:

$$MakeProperReturn \mathrel{\widehat{=}} (ReturnLoan \land OKMessage) \lor$$
$$ReturnLoanError$$

A.11 Making a reservation

Moving on, we write a schema which describes the making of reservation:

```
┌─MakeReservation ─────────────────────────────
│ ΔMusicLib
│ mem?                  : Person
│ record?               : Recording
├──────────────────────────────────────────────
│ mem?                  ∈ member
│ record?               ∈ ran held
│ ∀ c : Copy | c ↦ record? ∈ held •
│                       ∃ m : Person | m ≠ mem? • c ↦ m ∈ loan
│ loan'                 = loan
│ member'               = member
│ held'                 = held
│ reservation'          = reservation ∪ {record? ↦ mem?}
└──────────────────────────────────────────────
```

This has the preconditions:

• that the member is a member
• that the recording is one held by the library
• that all copies of this recording are out on loan to other members

The error schema for making reservations would be:

```
┌─ReserveError ─────────────────────────────────
│ ΞMusicLib
│ mem?                  : Person
│ record?               : Recording
│ reply!                : Response
├──────────────────────────────────────────────
│ (mem?                 ∉ member              ∨
│ record?               ∉ ran held            ∨
│ ∃ c : Copy | c ↦ record? ∈ held •
│                       c ∉ dom loan ∨ c ↦ mem? ∈ loan)
│ reply!                = errorOnReserve
└──────────────────────────────────────────────
```

The complete schema for making reservations will be:
$$ProperReservation \cong (MakeReservation \wedge OKMessage) \vee$$
$$ReserveError$$

A.12 Cancelling a reservation

To complete this particular scenario we write a schema which describes cancelling a reservation:

```
┌─CancelReservation ────────────────────────────────
│ ΔMusicLib
│ mem?              : Person
│ record?           : Recording
├────────────────────────────────────────────────────
│ record? ↦ mem?    ∈ reservation
│ loan'             = loan
│ member'           = member
│ held'             = held
│ reservation'      = reservation \ {record? ↦ mem?}
└────────────────────────────────────────────────────
```

This has the simple precondition that the reservation exists as a member of the set of reservations.

The corresponding error schema would be:

```
┌─CancelResError ───────────────────────────
│ ΞMusicLib
│ mem?              : Person
│ record?           : Recording
│ reply!            : Response
├─────────────────────────────────────────────
│ record? ↦ mem?    ∉ reservation
│ reply!            = errorOnReserve
└─────────────────────────────────────────────
```

We therefore have the complete schema for cancelling reservations:

$$ProperCancelRes \cong (CancelReservation \wedge OKMessage) \vee$$
$$CancelResError$$

A.13 Conclusion

As the reader will realise, the specification we have written in no way represents the complete picture of a music library. We have added schemas here which have not appeared in the main text of the book for the sake of balance. Similarly, we have omitted schemas that appear in the main text, since they represent views of the system which might not always be thought necessary. The view of the music library put forward in this appendix is a fairly simple view, which takes into account the usual operations of a library, missing out other operations which might not always be part of a library's requirements.

In a real situation various systems analysis techniques would be used to capture the requirements of the users as best they could. These would be presented in some form that the **Z** specification writer could work from. When this writer has completed the transformation of the natural language specification, s/he would normally have found a number of ambiguities, omissions and other problems in the original natural language version. They would then go back to the originators and seek clarification of these, returning to revise the **Z** specification in an iterative process.

This is the power of using a language like **Z**: to shine a searchlight on natural language specifications in order to expose problems for resolution before commitment to any hardware or software.

Answers to Exercises

Chapter 2 Mathematical Preliminaries

Exercise 1 page 24
(1) **false**
(2) **true**
(3) **true**
(4) **false**
(5) $A \cup B = \{1, 2, 3, 4, 6, 8, 10\}$
(6) $A \cap B = \{2, 4\}$
(7) $\{1, 2, 3, 4\}$
(8) $\{2, 3, 4\}$
(9) $\{1, 2, 3, 4, 5, 6, 7, 8, 10\}$
(10) $\{2\}$
(11) $\{1, 3\}$
(12) $\{1, 3, 4\}$

Exercise 2 page 33
(1) $\mathbb{P}C = \{\{\}, \{2\}, \{3\}, \{5\}, \{7\}, \{2, 3\}, \{2, 5\}, \{2, 7\}, \{3, 5\},$
$\{3, 7\}, \{5, 7\}, \{2, 3, 5\}, \{2, 3, 7\}, \{3, 5, 7\},$
$\{2, 5, 7\}, \{2, 3, 5, 7\}\}$
(2) $A \times C = \{\{1, 2\}, \{1, 3\}, \{1, 5\}, \{1, 7\}, \{2, 2\}, \{2, 3\}, \{2, 5\}$
$\{2, 7\}, \{3, 2\}, \{3, 3\}, \{3, 5\}, \{3, 7\}, \{4, 2\}, \{4, 3\},$
$\{4, 5\}, \{4, 7\}\}$
(3) $\#B = 5$
(4) $\#A = 4$
(5) 20
(6) $\{0, 1, 4, 9, 25, 36, 49, 64, 81\}$ (7) $\{1, 1/2, 1/3, 1/4\}$
(8) $Odds == \{x : \mathbb{Z} \mid x < 10 \bullet 2x + 1\}$
(9) $Evens == \{x : \mathbb{Z} \mid x < 10 \bullet 2x\}$
(10 $PerfectSquares == \{x : \mathbb{N}_1 \mid x < 11 \bullet x^2\}$

Chapter 3 Functions

Exercise 1 page 49
(1) (a) $\operatorname{ran} f = \{2, 6, 7, 8\}$, $\operatorname{ran} g = \{1, 2, 4, 8, 16, 32\}$,
$\operatorname{ran} h = \{0, 1, 4, 9\}$
(b) f, g and h
(c) f and g
(d) $\operatorname{dom} f^{-1} = \{2, 6, 7, 8\}$ $\operatorname{ran} f^{-1} = \{4, 7, 2, 9\}$
$\operatorname{dom} g^{-1} = \{1, 2, 4, 8, 16, 32\}$ $\operatorname{ran} g^{-1} = \{0, 1, 2, 3, 4, 5\}$
(2) Yes

Exercise 2 page 54
(1) (a) $f \oplus \{Cola \mapsto 35\}$
(b) f is no longer injective and f^{-1} ceases to exist
$\{The\ Celts \mapsto Enja\} \not\subseteq f$
(2) (a) $f: Title \to Artist$
$f \oplus \{The\ Celts \mapsto Enja\}$
$h \oplus \{The\ Celts \mapsto pop\}$
$g \oplus \{The\ Celts \mapsto 10\}$
(b) $g \oplus \{Dreamland \mapsto 8\}$

(3) (a) $\{(1, x), (2, x), (3, z)\}$ (b) No

(4)

```
┌─cube_op──────────────
│
│  cube : ℝ → ℝ
│ ──────────────────────
│  x : ℝ • cube x = x³
```

(5)

```
┌─Select ──────────────────────────
│  MaxSize : ℕ
│  MinSize : ℕ
│  Sieve : ℕ ↣ ℙ ℕ
│ ─────────────────────────────────
│  n : ℕ • MinSize ≤ #(Sieve n) ≤ MaxSize
```

Chapter 4 Relations

Exercise 1 page 61
(1) (a) y is the wife of x (b) y is shorter than x
(2) (a) *Sister_of* == {*Lynne* ↦ *John, Sue* ↦ *Mike, Mary* ↦ *David*}
   (b)*Uncle_of* == {*John* ↦ *Chris, John* ↦ *Matthew, Mike* ↦ *Paul*}
(3) (a) *Charge* == {5, 10, 20}
   (b) *Acceptable_Coins* == { {5, 5, 5} ↦ 15, {5, 10} ↦ 15,
       {5, 5, 5, 5} ↦ 20, {5, 5, 10} ↦ 20, {10,10} ↦ 20,
       {10,10,10} ↦ 30, {10, 20} ↦ 30, {5, 5, 5, 5, 5, 5} ↦ 30,
       {5, 5, 10, 10} ↦ 30, {5, 5, 5, 5, 10} ↦ 30,
       {5, 5, 5, 5, 5} ↦ 25, {10,10,5} ↦ 25,
       {10, 5, 5, 5} ↦ 25, {20, 5} ↦ 25}

Exercise 2 page 67
(1) (a) transitive   (b) symmetric and transitive
   (c) none of these properties   (d) symmetric and transitive
   (e) symmetric   (f) symmetric and transitive

Exercise 3 page 72
(1) $R : A \leftrightarrow B$ == {$a : A, b:B \mid a \in (a..e) \wedge b \in (1..20) \bullet a \mapsto b$}
(2) (a) (*Brother_of* ⨾ *Mother_of*)⁻¹ = {*Chris* ↦ *John, Paul* ↦ *Mike*}
   and (*Mother_of*⁻¹ ⨾ *Brother_of*⁻¹) = {*Chris* ↦ *John, Paul* ↦ *Mike*}
   (b) *Nephew_of*
(3) (a) *PowersOfTwo* ⁺== {2 ↦ 4, 4 ↦ 8, 8 ↦ 16, 16 ↦ 32, 2 ↦ 8,
                    4 ↦ 16, 8 ↦ 32}
   (b) R ⁺== {2 ↦ 4, 4 ↦ 8, 8 ↦ 4, 4 ↦ 2, 2 ↦ 8, 8 ↦ 2}
      R *== {2 ↦ 4, 4 ↦ 8, 8 ↦ 4, 4 ↦ 2, 2 ↦ 8, 8 ↦ 2, 2 ↦ 2,
          4 ↦ 4, 8 ↦ 8}

(4) (a) *Luton $\underline{R}$ Bedford, Bedford $\underline{R}$ Dunstable* hence
     Luton $\underline{R}$ Dunstable
     establishing the transitivity of the relationship;
     also, *Dunstable $\underline{R}$ Luton* establishing symmetry;
     finally *Luton $\underline{R}$ Luton* establishing reflexivity.
  (b) Equivalence classes: *{Hatfield, StAlbans, Hitchin}*,
                            {Luton, Bedford, Dunstable}

(5) Using given sets *ROOM , SESSION, COURSE*
(a) *book : ROOM $\leftrightarrow$ COURSE*
(b) domain restriction e.g. *laboratory $\lhd$ book*
(c) range restriction e.g. *book $\rhd$ Science*
(d) *make : SESSION $\leftrightarrow$ COURSE*
(e) *book $\,\mathbf{_9^o}\,$ make^{-1}*
(6) (a) *Birth : Person $\to$ Year*
A total function as every person has a year of birth.
(b) *Fate : Year $\twoheadrightarrow$ Sign*
This systems is surjective as every year has an animal sign.
(c) This solution is based on a composition from *Birth* to *Fate* so for the
    person *Tim*
     {Tim} $\lhd$ (Birth $\,\mathbf{_9^o}\,$ Fate)
(d) For *Tim* domain restriction will give the answer: *{Birth(Tim)} $\lhd$ Fate*
(e) After the birth of a person *Dominic : {Dominic $\mapsto$ 1993} $\cup$ Birth*
(f) Taking the members of the family as the set *Family :*
    # (Family $\lhd$ Birth $\,\mathbf{_9^o}\,$ Fate)$\rhd$ {Rat})

Chapter 5   An introduction to Z

Exercise page 90

(1) Answers to these may be found in appendix A, sections A.7 and
A.8

(2) The following schema introduces a set *artist* of type $\mathbb{P}$ *Person*, and a
relation *perform* of type *Person $\leftrightarrow$ Recording*. It also includes the
constraints that the people performing are a subset of the set *artist*, and
that the recordings participating in the relation are a subset of the
recordings held by the library. This allows for the possibility of
recordings being held without any information about the artists
involved: a situation which may arise when a recording has only
recently been acquired.

```
┌─ArtistIndex ──────────────────────────
│ MusicLib
│ artist              : ℙ Person
│ perform             : Person ↔ Recording
├───────────────────────────────────────
│ dom perform         ⊆ artist
│ ran perform         ⊆ ran held
└
```

(3) The following schema assumes that the recording in question has its artists listed in the index. Otherwise, it will give the empty set as output.

```
┌─WhoPerforms ──────────────────────────
│ ΞArtistIndex
│ record?             : Recording
│ artists!            : ℙ Person
├───────────────────────────────────────
│ record?             ∈ ran held
│ artists!            = perform~ (|{record?}|)
└
```

(4) As we state in appendix A, section A.6, we would only wish to add recordings when we add copies. Therefore, if we add a new recording, this must be done by adding at least one new copy, which will be of the new recording. We can insist that the recording is a new one by means of the following schema, which uses *AddCopy* from the appendix:

```
┌─AddRec ──────────────────
│ AddCopy
├──────────────────────────
│ record?        ∉ ran held
└
```

This does not show error conditions, which are more fully covered in later chapters.

Chapter 6 Predicate Calculus
Exercise page 108

(1) The truth table for ¬P ∨ ¬Q is:

P	Q	¬P	¬Q	¬P∨¬Q
T	T	F	F	F
T	F	F	T	T
F	T	T	F	T
F	F	T	T	T

a similar truth table for ¬(P ∨ Q) establishes the logical equivalence of the two expressions.

(2) (a) Rainy(*Monday*)
    (b) $\forall x : DaysInWeek \bullet Rainy(x)$
    (c) $\exists x : DaysInWeek \bullet Rainy(x)$
    (d) $\exists_1 x : DaysInWeek \bullet Rainy(x)$

(3) (a) **false**   (b) **true**
    (c) **false**   (d) **false**
    (e) **true**   (f) **true** - a tautology
    (g) **false** - a contradiction

(4)

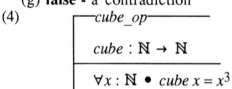

$$cube : \mathbb{N} \to \mathbb{N}$$
$$\forall x : \mathbb{N} \bullet cube\ x = x^3$$

Chapter 7 Z schema calculus

Exercise page 123

(1) An answer to this may be found in appendix A, section A.6

(2) The composition of two schemas will take the form:

$$MemberVanish \cong RemoveCopies \ \fatsemi \ RemoveMember$$

We first define the two schemas being composed. A similar one to the first, *RemoveCopy*, exists in appendix A, section A.8. We can write a schema like this to create a schema, *RemoveCopies*, as follows:

$$
\begin{array}{|l}
\hline
\text{\textit{RemoveCopies}} \\
\Delta\textit{MusicLib} \\
\textit{mem?} \quad : \textit{Person} \\
\hline
\textit{mem?} \qquad\qquad \in \textit{member} \\
\textit{held'} \qquad\qquad = \text{dom} \{ \textit{loan} \rhd \textit{mem?} \} \lhd \textit{held} \\
\textit{member'} \qquad\quad = \textit{member} \\
\textit{loan'} \qquad\qquad = \textit{loan} \\
\textit{reservation'} \qquad = \textit{reservation} \\
\hline
\end{array}
$$

The second schema *RemoveMember* is similar to the schema in appendix A, section A.7, *RemoveMem*, except that in this case we do not want the preconditions that the member has no loans or reservations outstanding. It would make the ensuing answer somewhat complex to proceed with these. We thus write a similar schema, *RemoveMember*:

$$
\begin{array}{|l}
\hline
\text{\textit{RemoveMember}} \\
\Delta\textit{MusicLib} \\
\textit{mem?} \qquad : \textit{Person} \\
\hline
\textit{mem?} \qquad\qquad \in \textit{member} \\
\textit{member'} \qquad\quad = \textit{member} \setminus \{ \textit{mem?} \} \\
\textit{held'} \qquad\qquad = \textit{held} \\
\textit{loan'} \qquad\qquad = \textit{loan} \\
\textit{reservation'} \qquad = \textit{reservation} \\
\hline
\end{array}
$$

For the sake of clarity, this answer does not consider non-standard or error conditions. We now go through the composition of *RemoveCopies* and *RemoveMember* using the steps described in the chapter.

(a) The revised version of the first schema of the composition, *RemoveCopies*, is labelled *RemoveCopies*["/ ']:

$$
\begin{array}{|l}
\hline
\text{\textit{RemoveCopies}["/ ']} \\
\textit{MusicLib} \; ; \; \textit{MusicLib"} \\
\textit{mem?} \quad : \textit{Person} \\
\hline
\textit{mem?} \qquad\qquad \in \textit{member} \\
\textit{held"} \qquad\qquad = \text{dom} \{ \textit{loan} \rhd \textit{mem?} \} \lhd \textit{held} \\
\textit{member"} \qquad\quad = \textit{member} \\
\textit{loan"} \qquad\qquad = \textit{loan} \\
\textit{reservation"} \qquad = \textit{reservation} \\
\hline
\end{array}
$$

(b) The revised version of the second schema, *RemoveMember*, is referred to as *RemoveMember*["/]:

```
┌─RemoveMember["/ ]──────────────────
│ MusicLib" ; MusicLib'
│ mem?          : Person
├───────────────────────────────────
│ mem?                ∈ member"
│ member'             = member" \ {mem?}
│ held'               = held"
│ loan'               = loan"
│ reservation'        = reservation"
└───────────────────────────────────
```

(c) We write the new schema, *MemberVanish*, which includes *RemoveCopies*["/ '] and *RemoveMember*["/].

```
┌─MemberVanish ──────────────────────────
│ ΔMusicLib
│ mem?              : Person
├────────────────────────────────────────
│ ∃MusicLib"   •
│          mem?        ∈ member
│          mem?        ∈ member"
│          held"       = dom { loan ▷ mem? } ◁ held
│          member'     = member" \ {mem?}
│          member"     = member
│          loan"       = loan
│          reservation" = reservation
│          held'       = held"
│          loan'       = loan"
│          reservation' = reservation"
└────────────────────────────────────────
```

The double primed variables have been hidden in the predicate using the existential quantifier statement.

(d) The double primed variables within the schema generated by step c) are eliminated by considering the equalities within the predicate:

```
┌─MemberVanish ──────────────────────────────┐
│ ΔMusicLib                                    │
│ mem?              : Person                   │
├──────────────────────────────────────────── │
│ ∃MusicLib″  •                                │
│         mem?      ∈ member                   │
│         held′     = dom { loan ▷ mem?} ◁ held │
│         member′   = member \ {mem?}          │
│         member″   = member                   │
│         loan″      = loan                     │
│         reservation″ = reservation            │
│         held′      = held″                    │
│         loan′      = loan                     │
│         reservation′ = reservation            │
└──────────────────────────────────────────────┘
```

The $\exists MusicLib''$ quantification can now be eliminated, since each double dashed variable is equal to one of the plain or single dashed variables. The quantification, therefore, carries no further useful information:

```
┌─MemberVanish ──────────────────────────┐
│ ΔMusicLib                                │
│ mem?              : Person               │
├──────────────────────────────────────── │
│ mem?              ∈ member               │
│ held′   = dom { loan ▷ mem?} ◁ held      │
│ member′             = member \ {mem?}     │
│ loan′               = loan                │
│ reservation′        = reservation         │
└───────────────────────────────────────────┘
```

This final schema *MemberVanish* is the composition of *RemoveCopies* and *RemoveMember*.

(3) The conditions are that all existential quantified variables are expressed in terms of *MusicLib* components and *copyref?*, and all these values satisfy *MusicLib'Predicate*.

The variables *member'*, *held'*, *loan'* and *reservation'* are already so expressed since they are part of the declaration of *MusicLib'* and have to satisfy its predicate. This leaves *mem!*, which can be expressed as a component of *MusicLib'*, if we add the constraint: *mem!* ∈ *member'*. This is an implicit constraint in the definition of *WhoHasCopy*. However, the process of simplifying the precondition has shown the need for this constraint explicitly. This illustrates again the power of **Z** in revealing facts about the system under investigation.

(4) The schema from chapter 5 is:

```
┌─AddNewMem ──────────────────
│ ΔMusicLib
│ mem?   :Person
├──────────────────────────────
│ mem?   ∉ member
│ member' = member ∪ {mem?}
│ held'   = held
│ loan'   = loan
│ reservation' = reservation
└──────────────────────────────
```

A precondition schema is started by writing:

```
┌─preAddNewMem ──────────────────
│ MusicLib
│ mem?   :Person
├──────────────────────────────
│ ∃MusicLib' •
│         mem?        ∉ member
│         member' = member ∪ {mem?}
│         held'       = held
│         loan'       = loan
│         reservation' = reservation
└──────────────────────────────
```

Conjuncts without any primed variables are then separated out:

```
┌─preAddNewMem ──────────────────
│ MusicLib
│ mem?   :Person
├──────────────────────────────
│ mem?   ∉ member
│ ∃MusicLib' •
│         member'     = member ∪ {mem?}
│         held'       = held
│         loan'       = loan
│         reservation' = reservation
└──────────────────────────────
```

Since we can state that the dashed variables are expressed in terms of *MusicLib'* components and that they are satisfied by *MusicLib'Predicate*, we write the final precondition schema:

```
┌─preAddNewMem ──────
│  MusicLib
│  mem?   :Person
├──────────────────────
│  mem?   ∉ member
└──────────────────────
```

Chapter 8 Finite Functions and Sequences

Exercise 1 page 132
(1) m
(2) $\langle\ n, o, p, q, r\ \rangle$
(3) $\langle\ \rangle$
(4) $\langle\ m, n,\ o, p, q\ \rangle$
(5) r
(6) $\langle\ \rangle$
(7) $\langle q\rangle$
(8) $\langle r ,q, p, o, n, m\ \rangle$
(9) a) $P\,(0)$ holds
          $P\,(s)$ holds for sequences
          $P\,(\langle x\rangle\ {}^\frown s\,)$ holds for $x{:}X$
    b) $P\,(\langle\ \rangle)$ holds
          $P\,(\langle x\rangle)$ holds for $x{:}X$
          $P\,(s)$ and $P(t)$ holds so also does $P\,(s\ {}^\frown\ t)$

Exercise 2 page 142
1) The sequence notation:
(a) Given type $Sign$ can then be used as seq$Sign$, defined as
$\langle Rat, Ox, Tiger, Rabbit, Dragon, Snake, Horse, Sheep, Monkey,$
   $Rooster, Dog, Boar\rangle$
   s = $(Fate) \circ t = \langle Frazer,\ Andy, Mike,\ Alan, Chris\rangle$
(b) $head\ s\ =\ \langle\ Frazer\rangle$
    $last\ s =\ \langle Chris\rangle$
(c) the Yin members of the group:
    $Fate \rhd \{Yin\}=\{Alan, Chis, Andy\}$
    $Fate \rhd \{Yang\}=\{Mike, Frazer\}$
    $s = \langle Frazer,\ Andy, Mike,\ Alan, Chris\rangle$
    $seqyin\ =\ s \upharpoonright \{Yin\}\ =\langle Andy, Alan, Chris\rangle$
(d) $seqyang\ =\ s \upharpoonright \{Yang\} = \langle Mike, Frazer\rangle$

(2) The given types [$CUSTOMER, SPOINT, STIMES$]
The functional relationships:

service_at = *CUSTOMER* → *SPOINT*
cus_service = *service_at* ⨾ *STIMES*
s: seq *CUSTOMER*

sp1; *sp2* : *CUSTOMER*   for sequences of customers waiting at points
sp1 and *sp2*.
tm1;*tm2* : *seq* $\mathbb{N}_1$ for sequences of waiting times at points *tm1*
and *tm2*.

Chapter 9   Introduction to bags

Exercise 1 page 150
(a) 3
(b) 2
(c) { *l* ↦ 2, *m* ↦ 5, *n* ↦ 8 }
(d) { *l* ↦ 2, *m* ↦ 1, *n* ↦ 2 }
(e) { *l* ↦ 16, *m* ↦ 12, *n* ↦ 20 }
(f) 20
(g) 0
(h) use *count* to show each element , *l*, *m*, *n* in *B* is less than the *count*
in *A*.

Exercise 2 page 154
(1) Given types - [*STUDENT*, *SUBJECT*]
bag *marks* = *STUDENT* ⇸ $\mathbb{N}$
maths, computing, french, design : bag *marks*
(a) a student's average mark
Average = (*count maths Fatima* + *count computing Fatima* ...)/
(#*SUBJECT*)
(b) average for a subject
subject_mean = (*count maths Fatima* + *count maths Tim* ...)/
(#*STUDENT*)
(2) Given type *GAME* , *Match1*, *Match2*, *Match3* of type bag *GAMES*,
(a) *Match1* = (*Jenny* ↦ 6, *Maureen* ↦ 6, *Ros* ↦ 3, *Lynne* ↦ 3)
  Match2 = (*Jenny* ↦ 5, *Maureen* ↦ 4, *Ros* ↦ 5, *Lynne* ↦ 4)
  Match3 = (*Jenny* ↦ 7, *Maureen* ↦ 2, *Ros* ↦ 7, *Lynne* ↦ 2)
(b) *count* (*Match1* ⊎ *Match2* ⊎ *Match3*) *Jenny*
(c) Zero (the number in a bag cannot be negative)-*count* (*Match1* ⊎ *Match*
(d) *count* (*Match1* ⊎ *Match2* ⊎ *Match3*)/ #*Match*

Chapter 10   Further Z examples

Exercise page 168

(1)

$$\begin{array}{|l}
\hline [X] \\\\
\quad squash : (\, \mathbb{N} \nrightarrow X) \nrightarrow \text{seq } X \\\\
\hline
(\forall fun : \mathbb{N} \nrightarrow X \;\bullet\; ((fun = \varnothing \wedge squash\, fun = \langle \rangle \,) \qquad \vee \\\\
\quad (\exists least : \text{dom } fun \mid (\,\forall m : \text{dom } fun \;\bullet\; least \leq m) \\\\
\qquad \bullet\; squash\, fun = \langle fun\, least \rangle \;\widehat{\;\;}\; squash\,(\{least\} \lhd fun))) \\\\
\hline
\end{array}$$

Here we have simply replaced the ordinary partial function symbol, $\nrightarrow$, by the finite partial function symbol, $\nrightarrow$, and removed the constraint which was needed to ensure finiteness.

(2)

$$\begin{array}{|l}
\hline RecordingList \\\\
\quad \Xi MusicLib \\\\
\quad reclist! : \text{seq } Recording \\\\
\hline
reclist! = placeinorder\,(\text{ran } held, inorder\,[Recording]) \\\\
\hline
\end{array}$$

(3)

$$\begin{array}{|ll}
\hline GenericReserveEnq\,[GRecording, GPerson] \\\\
\quad reserveMap & : GRecording \leftrightarrow GPerson \\\\
\quad heldMap & : GCopy \nrightarrow GRecording \\\\
\quad grecord? & : GRecording \\\\
\quad gmem! & : GPerson \\\\
\hline
\quad grecord? & \in \text{ran } heldMap \\\\
\quad gmem! & = reserveMap\,(\!|\{grecord?\}|\!) \\\\
\hline
\end{array}$$

(4) $IsHeld \triangleq [\; held : Copy \nrightarrow Recording \;;\; copyref? : Copy$
$\qquad\qquad\qquad \mid copyref? \in \text{dom } held \;]$

This should be normalised to:

$$\begin{array}{|ll}
\hline IsHeld \\\\
\quad held & : \mathbb{P}\,(Copy \times Recording) \\\\
\quad copyref? & : Copy \\\\
\hline
\quad held & \in Copy \nrightarrow Recording \\\\
\quad copyref? & \in \text{dom } held \\\\
\hline
\end{array}$$

The schema corresponding to ¬*IsHeld* would be *NotIsHeld*:

```
┌─NotIsHeld ──────────────────────
│  held        : ℙ(Copy × Recording)
│  copyref?    : Copy
├──────────────────────────────────
│  held        ∉ Copy ↠ Recording  ∨
│  copyref?    ∉ dom held
```

We thus have a surprising outcome in that, the *NotIsHeld* schema requires either that the item requested is not one of those held, or the alternative, that *held* is not a partial function at all. By negating the schema we have introduced a possibly undesirable side effect. In this case, the possibility that *held* is not a function might be excluded again by conjoining the schema *NotIsHeld* with another schema which would have embedded in it the Δ*MusicLib* schema. This contains the mandatory requirement that *held* is a partial function. However, the question as set does not mention this.

Chapter 11 An Introduction to Proofs in Z

Exercise page 179
(1) The initial state theorem for the music library is:

⊢ ∃ *MusicLib'* • *Init*

where:

```
┌─Init ──────────
│  MusicLib'
├─────────────────
│  member' = ∅
│  held'   = ∅
```

and

```
┌─MusicLib ─────────────────────────
│  member          : ℙ Person
│  held     : Copy ↠ Recording
│  loan     : Copy ↠ Person
│  reservation : Recording ↔ Person
├──────────────────────────────────
│  dom loan            ⊆ dom held
│  ran loan            ⊆ member
│  dom reservation     ⊆ ran held
│  ran reservation     ⊆ member
```

Replacing *MusicLib'* by its expansion in terms of predicates we have:

⊢ ∃ *member'* : ℙ*Person*; *held'* : *Copy* ↠ *Recording*;
  loan': *Copy* ↠ *Person*; *reservation* ' : *Recording* ↔ *Person*; •
  dom *loan'* ⊆ dom *held* ' ∧ ran *loan* '⊆ *member* ' ∧
  dom *reservation* '⊆ ran *held* ∧ ran *reservation* '⊆ *member'* ∧
  member' = ∅ ∧ *held'* = ∅

In this problem, the existential quantification is over *member'*, *held'*, *loan'* and *reservation'*. The last two conjunctions introduce an explicit value for these relationships, namely the empty set ∅. This enables us to discard the existential quantifier and replace by the empty set where appropriate. The final part of the proof then proceeds as indicated in chapter 11.

Bibliography

Diller, A. (1990). *Z- an introduction to the use of formal methods,*
John Wiley, Chichester.

Imperato, M.(1991). *An Introduction to Z,*
Chartwell-Bratt Ltd.

Ince, D.C. (1990). *An Introduction to Discrete Mathematics and*
Formal System Specification,
Oxford University Press, Oxford.

Lemmon, E.J. (1991). *Beginning Logic,* Chapman & Hall, London.

Lightfoot, D. (1991). *Formal Specification Using Z,*
The MacMillan Press.

McMorran, M., and Powell, S. (1993). *Z Guide for Beginners,*
Blackwell Scientific Publications.

Newton-Smith, W.H. (1985). *Logic: An Introductory Course,*
Routledge and Kegan Paul, London.

Potter, B., Sinclair, J . and Till, D. (1991). *An introduction to formal*
specification and Z,
Prentice Hall. Englewood Cliffs NJ.

Spivey, J.M. (1992). *The Z notation: A reference manual* (2nd edition)
Prentice Hall. Englewood Cliffs NJ.

Woodcock , J.C.P. and Loomes, M. (1988). *Software Engineering*
Mathematics, Pitman, London.

Wordsworth, J.B. (1992). *Software Development with Z,*
Addison -Wesley.

FUNCTIONS

Function	$f : A \rightarrow B$
Source	A
Domain	$\subseteq A$
Target	B
Range(range is a proper subset of target)	$\subseteq B$
Total Function	$f : A \rightarrow B$
Partial function	$f : A \nrightarrow B$
Injective function(one-to-one)	$f : A \rightarrowtail B$
Surjective function(onto)	$f : A \twoheadrightarrow B$
Bijective function(one-to-one correspondence)	$f : A \rightarrowtail\!\!\!\!\rightarrow B$
Composition forward	$g \,\fatsemi\, f$
backward	$g \circ f$
Inverse function	f^{-1}
Function Overriding	$f \oplus g$

RELATIONS

Relational image

The maplet notation $a \mapsto b$ is a graphical representation of the ordered pair (a, b). The formal definition of the image of a relation is given in Z notation as

$$R (\!| S |\!) == \{ \, x : X, y : Y \mid x \in S \wedge x \mapsto y \in R \bullet y \, \}$$

Inverse of a relation

Let R be a relation from A to B. The inverse of R denoted by R^{-1} or $R^{\sim}$ is the relation from B to A which consists of those ordered pairs which when reversed belong to R.

$$R^{-1} == \{ \, b : B; a : A \mid (a, b) \in R \bullet b \mapsto a \, \}$$

Projection of a relation

The projection function *first* will give the set of values corresponding to the first member of an ordered pair.

$first : (X \times Y) \rightarrow X$

While the projection function *second* will give the second member of an ordered pair.

$second : (X \times Y) \rightarrow Y$

Restriction of relations

$\lhd$ domain restriction
$\blacktriangleleft$ domain antirestriction
$\rhd$ range restriction
$\blacktriangleright$ range antirestriction

Types of relations

Let R be a binary relation on a set $A \times A$, then R is:

reflexive when for every $x \in A$, $x \underline{R} x$

symmetric when for every $x, y \in A$, $x \underline{R} y$ implies $y \underline{R} x$

transitive if for every x, y and z in A, $x \underline{R} y$ and $y \underline{R} z$ implies $x \underline{R} z$.

FINITE FUNCTIONS AND SEQUENCES

$\mathbb{F}X$	represents a finite subset of $\mathbb{P}X$
$X \nrightarrow Y$	represents finite partial functions between X and Y
$X \nrightarrowtail Y$	represents finite partial injections
$s : \mathbb{N} \rightarrow A$	represents the type of a sequence s of any set A
$s : \text{seq } A$	represents sequence s of type seq A
$\langle a, b, c, \dots \rangle$	represents a sequence of the elements of s
$\langle \rangle = \{\} = \varnothing$	represents the empty sequence
ran s	the set of objects forming a sequence s
$\text{seq}_1 A$	represents the sets of non-empty sequences of the elements of A
iseq A	the set of injective sequences with no repetitions
$rev\ s$	denotes the sequence which is the reverse of s.

decomposition

head s	denotes the first member of the sequence s
tail s	denotes all the elements, except the first member.
last s	the last element in a sequence s
front s	the elements of the sequence except the last member

concatenation

$\frown$	represents concatenation, forming a new sequence by joining two sequences in the correct order
$\frown /$	distributed concatenation, link together a series of sequences of the same type

selection

$s \upharpoonright A$	filtering a sequence by a set A
squash f	compaction of finite function into a sequence
$U \upharpoonleft s$	extraction of elements of an index U from a sequence
s prefix t	extraction from the front of a sequence

s suffix t extraction from the back of a sequence
s in t extraction where a sequence is found within a second longer sequence, combination of prefix and suffix

Laws

$$rev \langle \rangle = \langle \rangle$$
$$rev \langle x \rangle = \langle x \rangle$$
$$rev (rev\ s) = s$$

decomposition

$$s = (front\ s) \frown \langle last\ s \rangle$$
$$s = \langle head\ s \rangle \frown (tail\ s)$$

selection

$$s \upharpoonright A = squash\ (s \rhd A)$$
$$U \upharpoonleft s = squash\ (U \lhd s)$$
$$ran \langle x \rangle = \{x\}$$

Composition

$$f \circ \langle \rangle = \langle \rangle$$
$$f \circ \langle x \rangle = \langle f(x) \rangle$$

BAGS

$bag\ A == A \nrightarrow \mathbb{N}_1$ the type of bag A
$[\![a, b, b, c,\ c,\ c]\!]$ represents elements within bag brackets.
$[\![\ \ ]\!]$ represents the empty bag
$\sqsubseteq$ bag membership.
$x \in B$ represents object x in bag, B
$\sqsubseteq$ sub-bag membership
$B \sqsubseteq C$ represents B as a sub-bag of C
$count\ A\ x$ will give the frequency of x in bag A
$A \uplus B$ represents the bag union of A with B
$A \uplus B$ represents the bag difference of B from A
$n \otimes A$ represents the bag scaling of A by factor n
$items\ s$ will turn the sequence, s into a bag

Laws

$$A \uplus [\![\ ]\!] = A$$
$$n \otimes (A \uplus B) = n \otimes A \uplus n \otimes B$$
$$dom\ (B \uplus C) = dom\ B \cup dom\ C.$$
$$count\ (B \uplus C)\ x = count\ Bx + count\ Cx$$